The Modern Short Story in Peru

# THE MODERN SHORT STORY IN PERU

Earl M. Aldrich, Jr.

Madison, Milwaukee, and London, 1966

The University of Wisconsin Press

Published by
The University of Wisconsin Press
Madison, Milwaukee, and London
U.S.: Box 1379, Madison, Wisconsin 53701
U.K.: 26–28 Hallam Street, London, W.1

Printed in the United States of America by
Kingsport Press, Kingsport, Tennessee

Library of Congress Catalog No. 66–22860

To Betty

# PREFACE

THE PURPOSE of this book is to provide a chronological view of the modern short story from the time of its introduction into Peruvian literature at the turn of the present century through the early 1960's. The short story is examined as it evolves from a production studiedly cosmopolitan in nature to one oriented to the national scene and the distinctive rural areas of Peru. Finally, in its most recent stage the short story centers on the urban scene and on the more universal problems of modern man. In order to present this process in an orderly sequence, I have divided the study into five chapters, each corresponding to a significant phase in the development. I have chosen to highlight the major short story writers within each phase, giving biographical information and studying their narratives for type, content, significance within the period, and relationships to other periods. Minor writers and writers whose short story production is insignificant have been purposely omitted.

The technical developments of the short story are not nearly as clear-cut and easy to trace as the evolution of thematic concerns. There do occur certain advances and developments in technique, but the short story form as introduced by Clemente Palma and the *modernistas* is not basically altered by subsequent writers. However, in order to indicate the less obvious changes, I have included at the end of each chapter, with the exception of Chapter IV, a brief discussion of the five basic technical problems which every writer of fiction must face: (1) the narrator's point of view; (2) particularity, the extent to which the author will detail rather than generalize or sum up events; (3) order, the temporal structuring of events in the story; (4) economy, the extent to which the author implies, rather than specifies, elements of the story; (5) language, the special idiomatic usage and embellishments given to words. Some, undoubtedly, will object to dissecting literature in this fashion. It is, nonetheless, a method by which we can record differences and advances in technique. Hopefully, it will aid the reader in understanding more fully the evolution of the modern short story in Peru.

The primary sources of this study include the published short stories of all writers discussed—their works dispersed in newspapers and periodicals as well as those collected in book form. In addition, I have been fortunate to have at my disposal two unpublished manuscripts of Enrique López Albújar's early stories. Ciro Alegría was also kind enough to provide me with original manuscripts of several of his stories. A major portion of the historical material has been gleaned from Peruvian newspapers, journals, and magazines. Particularly important sources of background information for the early periods of the century are *Variedades, Colónida,* and *Amauta.* Much of the biographical material was taken from Peruvian newspapers and periodicals, such as *El Comercio, La Prensa, La Crónica, Cultura Peruana,* and *Mercurio Peruano.* Another principal source of biographical and background data was that of personal interviews with several of the writers.

English translations of the Spanish quotations have been provided for the benefit of those who do not read the language with facility. It is only fair, of course, to inform such readers that I have not been able to capture in all cases the exact flavor and style found in the original language; the subtle nuances of certain colloquial expressions proved to be particularly elusive. The original Spanish passages are included in a special section at the end of the book.

I am indebted to a number of people for their assistance in the preparation of this study: Professor Harvey L. Johnson of the University of Houston for his early interest and many helpful suggestions; Mr. James E. Plopper of the University of Wisconsin Extension Division for his careful reading of my drafts; Sr. Juan Mejía Baca, a Peruvian editor, and Dr. Alberto Escobar, of the Universidad de San Marcos, for their invaluable aid in securing research materials and arranging interviews. Finally, I wish to acknowledge the support granted by the Research Committee of the Graduate School of the University of Wisconsin from special funds voted by the State Legislature.

# CONTENTS

The Modern Short Story in Peru

# I

## THE BEGINNING
## OF THE MODERN
## SHORT STORY

DURING THE COURSE of the twentieth century, the short story has become the most cultivated and significant form of fiction in Peru. Many of the country's most distinguished men of letters, like Abraham Valdelomar, Enrique López Albújar, and Ventura García Calderón, have come into prominence through their production in the genre. In testimony to its continued importance, we need only look to the period since 1950 in which practically all of the emerging young writers use the short story as a vehicle for their literary efforts. The steady growth of the short story during the past sixty years stands out in sharp contrast to the relatively slow and irregular development of the Peruvian novel. This discrepancy has been explained both in psychological and economic terms: the unique predilection of the Peruvian for short fiction, the greater opportunity for authors to publish works of limited length in local periodicals, and simply the fact that most writers cannot afford the time required to write long novels. Whatever the reasons, the significant fact is that the modern short story clearly dominates twentieth-century Peruvian fiction and reflects Peru's major aesthetic and social currents.

Although the short story in Peru is a product of the present century, it has antecedents which date back to the pre-Conquest days of the Inca culture. The ancient Peruvians explained their origin, religion, and natural phenomena through myths which were passed from generation to generation by storytelling. When the Spaniards arrived in the sixteenth century, many of these stories were written down, some being preserved in well-known Spanish chronicles of the Conquest.

In the seventeenth century, another important precursor of the short story is El Inca Garcilaso de la Vega's *Comentarios reales,* published in two parts (1609 and 1616). This work has been studied primarily as a source of information for those interested in Inca culture; however, it is of equal significance for the student of literature. Garcilaso himself was an accomplished storyteller, and he included in his famous work many anecdotes which anticipate the modern story in their style and dramatic force.

*El lazarillo de ciegos caminantes,* published in 1773, is another noteworthy antecedent. Its relationship to the modern short story is also found in the lively anecdotes which the anonymous author uses in describing a trip from Montevideo to Lima via Buenos Aires, Salta, and Cuzco.

It is in the nineteenth century with its *costumbrista* sketches and *tradiciones* that we find the narratives which most closely anticipate the modern Peruvian short story. One of the very popular forms of fiction during the century was the *cuadro de costumbres,* a brief sketch which depicted, often in a satirical way, the life and manners of Peruvian society, particularly in Lima. Felipe Pardo y Aliaga (1806–68) and Manuel Ascencio Segura (1805–71) were outstanding writers of these narratives. Pardo, a member of the old Peruvian aristocracy, published some of his best *cuadros* in the periodical *El Espejo de mi Tierra.* Many of the vignettes cleverly satirize politicians of the day. Segura—different in background and approach but, in a sense, complementary to Pardo—was a soldier, and later a minor public official, who wrote light, spontaneous sketches. Segura is at his best when depicting the ambitions and dissatisfactions of the Peruvian middle class.

The greatest Peruvian literary figure of the nineteenth century and the most illustrious link in the narrative chain leading to the modern short story in Peru is Ricardo Palma (1833–1919). He originated a new literary form, the *tradición*, to use his own term. Vitally interested in the social and political history of Peru, he explored the rich collection of documents and manuscripts in the National Library. Roaming the streets and market places of Lima, he learned the traditional sayings and *coplas*. With rare talent, he used this material in fascinating narratives which combine humor, history, and imagination. In general, he followed a set structural formula in the *tradiciones*. Most of them are divided into three or more parts. In the first part, he introduces the legend or incident around which he weaves his decorative details. Then, having awakened reader interest, he drops narrative development to give historical background, thus lending a subtle quality of authenticity to the work. Finally, he picks up the thread of the narrative, at times racing to a rapid conclusion, other times pausing to add entertaining details. This new literary invention did not end with Palma, but was widely imitated in Peru and other Latin American countries.

While brief narratives can be found in all periods of Peruvian literature, it is only since the turn of the present century that the modern short story form has appeared in Peru. This relatively late introduction coincides, not surprisingly, with the tardy influence of *modernismo*, a literary movement which, though peculiarly American in its development, subsumes many of the major European artistic and moral preoccupations of the second half of the nineteenth century.[1] The *modernistas* are, naturally, well aware of prevailing *fin de siècle* themes and fictional forms. Their writings reveal a special interest in the brief narrative as it was developed by Poe, Maupassant, and others. They grasp the fundamental importance of the "unique" or "single effect," as Poe originally termed the principle; they understand that a short story is brief not merely because it contains comparatively few words, but also because it is deliberately compressed to gain a unity of impression by omitting non-essential elements. Thematically, the *modernistas'* stories reflect the currents of skepticism, pessimism, and irony so evident in the European literature of the time. Furthermore, in obvious reaction to the previous obsession of Peruvian fiction with local types and customs, they frequently seek their inspiration abroad. When local settings and characters are used, they are presented in such a way as to give the story a cosmopolitan appeal.

If the debut of the short story in Peru is directly related to the manifestations of *modernismo* there, its firm establishment can be largely attributed to the number of talented *modernista* prose writers active during this time. Clemente Palma, Abraham Valdelomar, Enrique López Albújar, and Ventura García Calderón head a long list of writers who initiated the modern short story in Peru during the last years of the nineteenth century and the first decade of the twentieth. This phenomenon is the more noteworthy when one remembers that *modernismo* was, essentially, a poetic movement.

Although a number of writers participated in the introductory phase of the modern short story in Peru, it is Clemente Palma who deserves to be singled out for special study not only because of the early appearance of his narratives, but also because he is the most consistent and complete representative of the complex *fin de siècle* spirit. Ironically, however, the nature and fundamental importance of his contribution to Peruvian fiction have never been fully understood or appreciated because he has remained in the shadow of his illustrious father, Don Ricardo. Almost from the beginning of his career, well-meaning critics added to the eclipse with their references to his literary heritage. Miguel de Unamuno's remarks in a prologue to the first edition of Clemente Palma's *Cuentos malévolos* are typical of the tendency to view his works in the light of his father's achievements:

My esteemed friend: I have just read your book *Cuentos malévolos* which you have been kind enough to let me see before releasing it for publication. Both the prestige of your illustrious father, Don Ricardo, whose literary talent has given us so many moments of pleasure, and the fact that you are a young man have moved me to read your stories promptly and with interest. I particularly wanted to see if that saying "chip-off-the-old-block," and other similar expressions of which there are so many, would prove true in your case. I assure you that my expectations have not been disappointed.* [2]

Peruvian critics similarly discouraged serious study of the man and his work with comments of the same nature.[3] Thus, an objective appraisal of his position in the history of Peruvian fiction is long overdue.

Clemente Palma was born in Lima in 1875. Little of note has been recorded about his childhood and adolescence other than that he studied at prominent primary and secondary schools in the capital. In 1892 he enrolled at the University of San Marcos and received his Doctor of Letters degree in 1897. From 1891 to 1902, he worked in the National Library, which was then under his father's direction. In 1902 he went to Barcelona as Peruvian Consul, remaining until 1904 when he returned to Lima, again to work in the National Library. In 1911 he was elected a representative to Congress and held that post until 1930, when he was exiled to Chile for a short time. Fortunately, the subsequent years were relatively peaceful, and he was able to devote himself to both personal literary pursuits and public service until his death in 1946.

Much of Palma's time after returning to Peru in 1904 was dedicated to journalism. He immediately began writing theatrical reviews for *El País* and in 1905 was one of the founders of *Prisma*, an elegant, but short-lived, literary journal. In 1908 Palma founded the well-known periodical *Variedades,* which he published until 1930. At the same time, he founded the daily newspaper *La Crónica* and was associated with it until

* For original Spanish passages, see pages 163 ff.

1938. In summing up his journalistic career he makes special reference to the number and variety of articles which he contributed to both national and foreign journals. Besides works of fiction and criticism, he published more than a thousand essays and editorials on non-literary topics.[4]

Palma's first major work, and undoubtedly his most significant one, was *Cuentos malévolos,* a book of twelve short stories published in 1904, when he was Peruvian Consul in Barcelona. The narratives had appeared previously in various Peruvian magazines and newspapers beginning in the late nineties. Their appearance in book form is especially noteworthy since they constitute the first published collection of modern Peruvian short stories. A second edition of *Cuentos malévolos* with eight new stories added to the original twelve was published in Paris in 1923, with a prologue by Ventura García Calderón.[5] *Historietas malignas,* published in Lima in 1924, was Palma's third and last collection of stories.[6] The book contains four selections, all of which had formerly appeared in periodicals, one having been published as early as 1897.

In all these works, Palma displays a remarkable freedom in his choice of settings and characters. Russian, French, North American, Norwegian, and German protagonists play out their roles in a wide variety of settings. In "El día trágico" (*Cuentos malévolos*), the hero is an American engineer who lives in Lima. "Mors ex vita" (*Historietas malignas*) takes place in an unnamed city, and the protagonists are German and Norwegian. Palma seems to be demonstrating that the action of his tales could unfold any place in the world and that his characters could be of any nationality. Time, on the other hand, is more strictly limited. Palma is primarily concerned with the current scene, so that even when he projects temporally backward or forward for his plot, the point of reference is always the present, and the basic theme is inspired by prevailing *fin de siècle* currents.

The contemporary mood was, in fact, essentially pessimistic, reflecting the anguished reactions of many intellectuals to the disturbing implications of the scientific and technological advances of the age—advances which showed that the relation of human life to the scheme of the universe was frighteningly more complex than anyone had imagined. Anatole France spoke for many of the finest minds of the time when he observed: "We have eaten of the fruits of the tree of science, and there remains in our mouths the taste of ashes." [7] These disillusioned men saw the rapid advance of knowledge as a curse because it had stripped away cherished illusions about God and man without offering a shred of consolation in return. Their responses—or more accurately, their defenses— took the form of escapism, skepticism, mockery, blasphemy, or a superior detachment; but these recourses tended to underscore rather than conceal the gravity of the spiritual wounds. With few exceptions, Palma's short stories give evidence of the same malady. They link him to those French writers, often designated as decadents, who not only despaired over the stupidity of modern civilization and the horror of existence, but also explored unabashedly the paradises of hashish and the secrets of the demon world in their efforts to exploit all the ironic potentialities latent in that unhappy situation.

Palma had more than a superficial knowledge of the French decadent writers and their ideas. In 1897 he published a controversial doctoral dissertation entitled "Filosofía y arte" [8] dealing with such subjects as atheism, androgyny, and Satanism, with special emphasis on Joris Karl Huysmans' treatment of those matters in *Là-Bas*, a notorious decadent novel. Even more revealing is *Excursión literaria* (1894), a little known booklet consisting of ten articles which had been published separately in the newspaper *El Comercio*.[9] Despite his lack of historical perspective, Palma shows in this work a remarkable comprehension of the whole concept of decadence and its importance to *modernismo*. Moreover, he sees clearly that the common ground for all the pessimistic writers and thinkers of the day, no matter what their label—decadent, symbolist, realist, naturalist, or blasphemer—is precisely their despair over the great dilemma of modern civilization: the contrast between appearance and reality, between ideal and achievement, between the needs of civilized man and the exigencies of his reason.

The extent to which Palma shared the metaphysical concerns of the decadent writers is most evident in his short story production. In cruelly ironic narratives which flaunt his skepticism while betraying his despair, he mocks sacred beliefs, derides traditional morality, and questions the value of virtue in modern society. "Una historia vulgar" (*Cuentos malévolos*) is one of several stories designed to ridicule naïve pretensions concerning the natural goodness of man and the hope for humanitarian progress. The plot is simple. Ernesto, a young innocent in a world of perversity, persists in his blind faith in mankind and in the romantic concept of ideal love, despite the warnings of his worldly-wise companion, Louis. Ultimately, his fondest illusions are shattered, and he is driven to suicide by the grotesquely perverse conduct of a girl whom he had idealized. The implications of the narrative are clear: Whether man likes it or not, he is, by a quirk of cosmic irony, born into a jungle of evil where a cruel struggle for survival goes on continually at all levels. Those who do not understand and adapt themselves to these conditions must pay the price. Had not Darwin's observations made all this painfully clear? Louis, the cynical sophisticate who tries to alert Ernesto to the folly of his naïve viewpoint, sees him as an anachronism in modern society, a person curiously out of step with reality:

The kindly Ernesto did not believe in evil, stating that all men and women were essentially good. Furthermore, he thought that any evil which, by chance, did show itself in them was of a purely temporary nature—a sort of passing crisis. . . . Evil, according to him, was an abnormal state which could be likened unto drunkenness or sickness and which would disappear quickly without leaving any scars. (p. 40)

Following Ernesto's tragedy, Louis is able, therefore, to remark with detached resignation that the victim's fate was inevitable because of the weaknesses represented by his noble spirit, unwarranted optimism, and trusting nature.

In "El quinto evangelio," "Parábola," and "El hijo pródigo" (*Cuentos malévolos*), Palma not only elaborates on his disquieting view of the world as a cruel, evil place where the upright and trusting are quickly destroyed, but also mocks the fundamental hope of Christianity—salvation through Christ. These stories reveal as clearly as any works of the period the pathetic dilemma faced by those sensitive to the poverty of existence and incapable of believing in that which would give solace. The setting for "El quinto evangelio" is Calvary. Christ is in the agonies of death, and Satan pays him a final, triumphant visit:

Nazarene, you have been a deluded visionary. You thought that you were going to redeem us, but you have not succeeded. His Majesty Sin reigns today as omnipotent as before—and even more so. Original sin, whose stain you tried to wash away, is our most delightful and precious possession. (p. 82)

You wanted to save mankind but you can't, because the salvation you offer is death. Man wants to live, and life is my essence. . . . Don't you know, oh unfortunate martyr, that I am flesh, desire, knowledge, passion, and curiosity? I am all the energies and stimuli of life. I am everything that makes man want to live. (p. 79)

Christ cannot even survive, let alone carry out his mission, in a world where man's strongest drives are selfish and evil. He dies—an innocent victim rather than the savior of mankind.

The extravagant idea of evil as the dynamic force which gives man a reason for existence is further developed in "Parábola." Christ returns to earth a second time and finds mankind even more evil than during his first visit. At the insistence of a hermit, he reluctantly agrees to eliminate for a time the scourges of sickness, poverty, and hate. But the earthlings are so unhappy with this "blessing" that they beg for the return of the maladies. In the world Palma depicts here, disease, evil, and strife are man's most prized possessions. By a grotesque inversion of values, the abnormal, the anti-natural, and the corrupt assume normality and vitality. The goodness and health embodied in Christian ideals are irrelevant to man, and Christ's message is lost. In "El hijo pródigo," Palma traces this concept to its logical conclusion. God finally forgives Satan who returns to occupy his former place in the heavenly kingdom. However, with the removal of his evil influence, the universe loses its *raison d'être* and disintegrates into chaos. Despite all the illusions which man had created through the ages about himself and his environment, it had actually been the negative force of evil, as personified by Satan, that had made life evolve.

A feeling of decay and impending doom runs as an undercurrent through these narratives, particularly the last three. Palma was, in fact, much influenced by the idea of modern corruption, the concept of a society suffering the pangs of moral decadence, the haunting thought of a civilization on the verge of collapse—concerns which became increasingly widespread during the last half of the nineteenth century and the early years of the twentieth.[10] On occasion, his expressions of this attitude are especially graphic, but none more so than in the following passage from "La leyenda de hachisch" which purports to be the hallucination of a man under the influence of drugs. It is, rather, a symbolic portrayal of a corrupt world, a sort of Darwinian nightmare in which the base, the unhealthy, and the abnormal have assumed the ascendancy.

The tangled tops of strange trees, their trunks covered with pustules, could be seen everywhere. The air had a foul odor like that of a hospital room occupied by patients suffering from

gangrene. Birds with purulent bodies moved about feebly, emit-
ting pitiful chirping sounds. Animals crippled by elephantiasis
crossed our path haltingly; their skin was mangy, their sunken
flanks seemingly in the process of being eaten away by a relentless
disease. The flowers, hardly opened, fell dying on the unhealthy
turf, their petals burning with a violent fever, their stamens
quivering and writhing with intense pain. . . . A lioness and her
cubs stretched out on the road. Green flies swarmed on the
pustules which covered her feeble body. . . . And as the poor
beast lay there panting and whimpering, her starving cubs, so
skinny their backbones seemed about to break through the skin,
tried desperately to take nourishment from her empty, flaccid
teats which gave forth nothing but vitiated blood. (pp. 141–42)

In Schopenhauerian fashion, Palma diagnoses mankind's condition as hopeless. He offers no healing for the sick, no
compensation for the weak, and no reward for the righteous.
For those who wish to be strong, he advocates pessimism; in a
decaying universe, it is the only force which can keep man
from vain hopes and false expectations.

The close link between Palma and the French decadents
becomes even more apparent when we study the heroes of his
stories—cynical, bored, worldly-wise creatures with perverse
desires and jaded appetites, whose bizarre activities are
symptomatic of the pessimism and despair of the time. They
pale, to be sure, beside that great archetype, the Duc des
Esseintes.[11] They are not even as advanced in their degener-
acy as some of the lesser heroes of *Monsieur de Phocas, Isis,* or
*Le vice supreme.*[12] Nevertheless, they display many of the
most salient traits of the decadent sensibility: skepticism,
detachment, disillusionment, unhealthy curiosity, and a remarkable capacity for ingenious self-torment.

The cult of artificiality is a fundamental characteristic of
decadence and decadent heroes. In a sense, it is a reaction
against Rousseau's idealization of nature, a reaction characterized by a self-conscious emphasis, even a glorification, of
any tastes which could be considered abnormal and anti-

natural. The decadent hero's obsessive identification with artificiality leads him into the most extravagant perversions—experimentation with drugs, Satanism, sexual excesses—in short, any activity or pose which would violate nature and provide new sensations.[13] In "El hijo pródigo," Palma refers to these heroes who seem driven by an inner force to taste of every forbidden fruit, but always to be denied lasting satisfaction, as disturbed products of the *fin de siècle* who take pleasure in everything that "is bizarre or that excites our already jaded and exhausted nervous systems" (p. 97).

His most noteworthy cultivators of artificiality are Marcario and Feliciano, the heroes of "El príncipe Alacrán" and "Un paseo extraño" (*Cuentos malévolos*). Both consider their artificial pursuits as temporary means of escape from the vulgarity and unhappy reality of contemporary life. Marcario relies mostly on drugs, while Feliciano, a somewhat more inventive fellow, is not averse to using the latest mechanical devices to satisfy his craving for the anti-natural.[14] Of special interest is Feliciano's experiment with diving equipment since it recalls some of the extravagant activities of Huysmans' hero who found sitting in a bath of salt water and watching mechanical fish swim about in an aquarium filled with artificial weeds preferable to visiting the seashore.

Feliciano is at first content to use his underwater equipment in the bathtub which he makes his nightly resting place. Dressed in his diver's suit, he submerges himself in the water and observes at length the eerie reflections of light in the room. He is also fond of agitating the surface of the water so that the objects about him appear in fascinatingly distorted shapes, some seeming to writhe in an infernal dance, others looming up like frightening monsters. The sensations he experiences are unusual, but he soon tires of this activity and decides to use his equipment in a more bizarre experiment: a trip through the city sewer system. The idea, of course, is entirely in keeping with the decadent sensibility since it gratifies the desire to exalt the grotesque and abnormal. Obviously, the more jaded the appetite, the rarer and more shocking the sensation must be. The following passage, which describes part of the journey, shows the emphasis on the monstrous and the unnatural:

His entrance caused a real turmoil. Millions of red cockroaches began to move about. . . . Feliciano had to go through some areas where the walls had crumbled away, forming small mounds of mud and stone. Toads infested these places as did snakes and large worms which coiled at Feliciano's feet or writhed in the agonies of death when he stepped on them. (pp. 192–93)

In another passageway, he spotted what appeared to be a small animal about the size of a fist. Directing his lantern toward it, he discovered that it was an enormous spider in whose belly a humming bird could have fit. The spider stared at him, its poisonous eyelets flashing like the tips of eight arrows soaked in curare. Its hairs bristled, and the excited palpitation of its thorax could be seen as it prepared, like a fighter, to do battle. . . . In another place he found a pair of toads whose large mouths seemed fixed in an eternal smile, while the expressions of their eyes gave the impression that they were lost in dreams of stupid voluptuousness. . . . Feliciano gave them a kick. They landed in the water and sank happily, finally alighting on another stone where they continued their love affair. (pp. 193–94)

An unexpected attack by sewer rats forces Feliciano to discontinue his subterranean search for new sensations, but he returns home satisfied for the moment by his experience. His reaction is reminiscent of Des Esseintes' abnormal response to receiving nourishment by enemas which he finds delightfully anti-natural rather than loathsome or repellent.[15]

Regarding sexual perversions, it must be noted first that Palma has little to say on the matter, and second, that his allusions to it are delicate. However, this does not mean that he avoids the subject. "La leyenda de hachisch" (*Cuentos malévolos*), a story in which he makes reference to abnormal sexual practices, is a case in point: "We thought of ourselves

almost as androgynes as we experienced together the mysteries of the night united in an intimate asexual fraternity" (p.
137). The narrator shares this relationship with Leticia whose
body "had the delicate purity of a crystallized virginity, the
childish charm and gracefulness of arrested adolescence" (p.
138). Ultimately, their unnatural affair contributes to the girl's
death:

Our madness was bound to be the death of her; and so it was. Her
body . . . was born for a bourgeois, methodical, serene, healthy
kind of love, not for the perverse, restless, and extenuating type of
relationship to which our minds filled with unhealthy curiosity, our
imaginations bubbling with daring fantasies, our nervous systems
always eager for new and shocking sensations had driven us. (p.
137)

This passage is significant because of the clear implication that
death was to be expected, since the practice of the artificial
and perverse is a contradiction of nature. Such an implication
underscores an essential paradox. Though the decadent hero
pursues artificiality with persistence and ostentation, he never
quite gets around to denying the tenets of Rousseau. In his
excellent study of the idea of decadence, Carter elaborates on
the paradox as follows:

The decadents, even when they refused to live by Rousseau's
gospel, never denied its truth. They were like unfrocked priests
celebrating the Black Mass—perfectly aware that their cult was
blasphemous. They accepted Nature as the norm, and primitivism
as synonymous with virtue. They admitted, either tacitly or
enthusiastically (depending on the individual writer's desire to
shock and astonish), that anything different, anything civilized or
"artificial," was *a priori* unnatural and depraved. From the very
beginning, decadent sensibility is thus self-consciously perverse;
and its cult of the artificial distinguishes it sharply from Romanticism, whatever traces of depravity may be found in certain
Romantics.[16]

The narrator of Palma's tale does not stop at the death of
Leticia. Rather, he resorts to drugs to further gratify his

senses. In his opium-inspired delirium, he is led on a symbolic journey by a guide who represents that ultimate and unattainable fulfillment of all decadent desires. At the end, she flees, leaving him to his never-to-be-satisfied search, the inevitable fate of all decadent heroes.

It follows that boredom is the bane of a decadent hero's existence, his constant companion, goading him into perversion and sadism; but since perversion and sadism, once experienced, lose their savor, he falls prey again to ennui, and so the cycle goes. However, the decadent hero approaches life for the most part on an intellectual, rather than a sentimental, plane and is able, therefore, to be almost logical in his manias. He explains his unnatural emotions and actions in the most matter-of-fact way, frequently with more than a hint of condescension in his tone.

An analysis of the imperious protagonists in "Los canastos" and "Idealismos" (*Cuentos malévolos*) reveals the typical pattern of ennui and sadism. Marcof, the hero of the first narrative, displays his contemptuous spirit and completely self-centered attitude in the opening paragraph by stating that if one must choose between doing a kind deed which will soon be forgotten by the beneficiary and a cruel act which will long be remembered the latter is always preferable. The setting is a wintry Russian evening. Admittedly bored and in search of stimulus, Marcof is walking along a narrow bridge. Ahead he sees Vassielich, a partially deaf teamster who is returning homeward, his cart loaded with twenty baskets of fish which have been consigned to him for sale in the market next day. Suddenly, the cord which holds the baskets on the cart breaks, and one falls into the water. Vassielich continues across the narrow bridge, unaware that his precious cargo is slipping, a basket at a time, into the swirling water below. Instead of warning the poor man, Marcof remains silent, watching the misfortune with intense pleasure. For the moment, his boredom has been relieved by his passive, but nonetheless cruel, participation in the drama. He has experienced a new sensation, a fresh titillation of his jaded senses, which is made exquisitely and perversely more acute when he hurries to inform Vassielich of his loss and thereby is able to enjoy observing close-up the unfortunate's reaction. Finally, he stays true to character by coolly and cynically analyzing his own actions as follows: "To be sure, Vassielich, a good fellow who had never done me any harm, was going to suffer greatly from the misfortune. But, so what? Did I lose anything because of Vassielich's disaster? No, on the contrary, I was pleasantly diverted while crossing that bridge which, by the way, is one hundred meters long" (p. 3).

The nameless hero of "Idealismos" is more active in his search for sadistic pleasure, but the same motivation and the same attitude are evident. He decides to kill his fiancée, but in no ordinary manner. He calculatedly instills in her a desire for death, thereby experiencing a thrill of power from slowly destroying another human being through an act of will. Like Marcof, he is deliberately perverse and delights in proclaiming his superiority over those who might be disgusted by his twisted views.

Both decadent heroes have achieved a perfect degree of self-preoccupation. As in the case of Des Esseintes, their only consideration in life is the temporary satisfaction of their abnormal cravings; nothing else, no one else, matters. They argue that their sadistic activities are perfectly justified. In fact, through an ironic inversion of values, they are able to assume a feeling of self-righteousness. The hero of "Idealismos" speaks of his deed as an act of liberation for the victim, an act of love performed with nobility and honor, while Marcof feels that he has helped in some way to re-establish the equilibrium of nature.

But the decadent is not a happy man. He lives with a gnawing sense of personal and social decay. Paradoxically, he abhors the fact that civilization is depraved, while, at the same

time, he takes a perverse pleasure in its very depravity.[17]
Though dismayed by a world where the old absolutes have
been destroyed, the romantic hero could find some measure of
solace in nature or ideal love; the decadent must live with
chronic dissatisfaction. In a sense, his flaunting of perverted
values is an anguished protest against the way things are; yet
he is absolutely resigned to the idea that nothing will ever
change for the better. On the other hand, he is never pompous
and he does have a certain ironic sense of humor.

Palma's decadent hero par excellence, the one who best
expresses the complex attitude of despair and cynicism at the
incongruous spectacle of modern civilization, is the narrator of
"El hombre del cigarrillo" (*Historietas malignas*). Throughout
his licentious life, he has gorged himself on all of the
perversions available in the vice-ridden metropolises of the
world. Having reached middle age, he is surfeited and thus
decides, rather lethargically, to commit suicide. From his
thoughts on the subject, however, we see that he anticipates
this act for the strange new sensation he will experience
rather than because of any desperate need to escape from life: [18]

> After a rapid and calm examination of the various means of
> committing suicide, I decided on hanging. I had heard that those
> who employed this method had a very pleasant death. Moreover, I
> had been assured that during those last moments while dancing at
> the end of the rope, one experienced a positively delectable
> sensation. (p. 62)

At this point, Palma gives an original twist to the Faust theme.
The narrator, who has purchased a rope and retired to the
forest, is intercepted by the Devil who offers him everything
from riches to the peace of forgetfulness if he will desist from
his suicide plan and surrender his will. In the course of
conversation, it becomes apparent that man through his own
evil ingenuity has invented an artificial means of achieving the
wicked realization of every temptation Satan can offer. The
hero's sometimes condescending, sometimes mocking, refusals

give a striking picture of his complete cynicism. He laughs at
the Devil's offer of forgetfulness, for example, pointing out
that man can assume such a state at any time through the use
of alcohol. Even the Devil's promise of supreme knowledge
and wisdom is dismissed with scornful skepticism:

Believe me, I am genuinely grateful for your unselfish interest in
urging me to postpone the aerial dance with which I propose to
put an end to my checkered career. I also regret very much
having to refuse that ancient offer which you made, on a previous
occasion, in the Garden of Eden. I refer, of course, to that fruitful
feast from the tree of the knowledge of good and evil which gave
a serious case of indigestion not only to our first parents but also to
Raimundo Lulio and that bunch of alchemists in the Middle Ages.
But why summarize, or rather, why try to encompass in a single
whole all the knowable and the unknowable when slowly but
surely we are emptying that tree of paradise? . . . The fact of
the matter is that little by little, during the course of the centuries,
all the veils will be drawn, and all the truths will be discovered
until we reach the ultimate truth which most likely will reveal that
everything was a lie. (pp. 78–79)

The story is brought to an ironic close when it is suggested
that civilization has reached a point where Satan is as
meaningless as God. Completely crushed by the resignation
and cynicism of the decadent hero, the Devil takes the rope
and hangs himself.

In the opening lines of "Las mariposas" (*Cuentos malévolos*), a story dedicated to his daughter, Palma characterizes
his own narratives as "flowerings of my unrestrained skepticism . . . stories which have their inspiration in the lowest
depths of the human spirit . . . stories of abnormal and
twisted passions, stories of misguided fantasy, of bitter and
resigned irony" (pp. 267–68). And certainly, the vivid reflection of *fin de siècle* pessimism and anguish constitutes one of
their most significant elements. Of equal importance, however,
are the technical considerations which shaped the writing of
these stories. Reference was made earlier in the chapter to the

*modernistas'* concern with unity of impression. We may object today to the oversimplification in Poe's pronouncement of "single effect," but at the same time it is obvious that it was conscientiously applied as a general guiding principle. Palma, in particular, made it a fundamental aspect of his short story technique.[19] But other principles also guided him, and in order to consider them as concisely as possible we shall examine his works in the light of five basic technical problems which confront every short story writer: the narrator's point of view, particularity, order of events, economy, and language usage.[20]

Palma relies almost exclusively on first person narration; however, within this point of view, he is able to achieve a rich variation. In such stories as "Los canastos" and "La granja blanca" (*Cuentos malévolos*), the narrator-protagonist recounts his own experiences, thereby giving the impression that the author and narrator are one. He also uses subterfuges, such as listening to the hero's telling of a personal experience ("Los ojos de Lina" in *Cuentos malévolos*) or recording verbatim what he has purportedly found in a diary ("Una historia vulgar"). In the latter story, a further dimension of viewpoint is achieved by having the diary keeper report what happened to a close friend so that he becomes, in effect, a first person witness. On two other occasions, "Un paseo extraño" and "Mors ex vita" (*Historietas malignas*), Palma also utilizes the narrator-witness, a lesser character who records not only his own actions but those of the protagonists.

The most interesting narrative in respect to point of view is "Vampiras" (*Cuentos malévolos*) in which Palma, using first person narration, skillfully weaves a story within a story. The narrator-protagonist, who is suffering from a mysterious malady, visits a physician and tells him his story. During the course of the visit, the doctor interrupts to tell the story of another patient who has suffered from a similar sickness. Following the doctor's account, which has the unity and dramatic interest of a complete story in itself, the original narrator takes up the thread of his own independent story which gains in richness from the preceding account. Throughout the narrative, the first person viewpoint never changes, but the position of the narrator does. Whereas the patient tells of his personal experience and discovery, the doctor, as a narrator witness, recounts the experience and discovery of another. Point of view is skillfully exploited here to give the narrative a more complex and interesting structure.

Limiting the point of view to a first person witness can be very effective since the story thus approximates a special condition of drama in which the audience, viewing the situation from the outside, must infer a great deal of the action. At the same time, however, the narrator's logically limited viewpoint and natural fallibility are difficult to maintain. In "Mors ex vita," where such a point of view is adhered to most extensively, Palma tries to squelch any unreal idea of omniscience by supplying testimony from other sources to support his narrator's accurate inferences about matters which he might not be expected to know. Unfortunately, these efforts also make for an overly lengthy and stilted narrative.

Palma is at his best when writing from the viewpoint of the narrator-protagonist. "Los canastos" and "La granja blanca," two outstanding stories, are good examples of this technique. In both cases, the protagonists are controversial men who express unnaturally cruel and bizarre attitudes. To provide an exterior analysis of them would be an easy way of supplying explanatory material, but it would also make the characters less convincing. Their opinions must be stated with a personal conviction which shocks the reader and gives him a direct view of their mentality. In both stories Palma accomplishes this goal with the skillful use of first person.

Particularity, or the extent to which the writer will treat the elements of the story in detail as opposed to summarizing and generalizing them, is a fundamental consideration. Particularizing, especially in the form of dialogue scenes, may be the source of dramatic force for the story. On the other hand, brevity is also of utmost importance. Austin McGiffert Wright's observations on the particularity of dramatic action make the problem of time very clear:

A dramatist does not have the narrator's privilege of generalizing a number of events (e.g., "Luisa used china everyday . . .") . . . . Dramatic action is particularized in two senses. In the first place, it is unique: every event is a single event that happens at one moment in time, no matter how many similar undepicted events may be assumed to have occurred at other moments. In the second place, it is coherent: not only does time move forward, but it moves forward without skips. As long as the curtain is up, all the components of a developing action, all the particulars in a time sequence, must be revealed.[21]

In this respect, the short story writer is less restricted, but he still must select his particularized scenes and use a method of summary and generalization which together will achieve both dramatic force and proper brevity. Palma's solution to the problem is uncomplicated and efficient. He carefully intersperses a limited number of dialogues, which have the effect of dramatic scenes, with the narrative passages. These dialogues are coherent and detailed, with well-defined beginnings and endings. Lead-ins are not omitted; every question asked receives a specific answer. While the dramatic scenes are thus fully developed, their use is restricted by the need for brevity. In most stories there are only two or three dialogue scenes. "Los canastos," for example, is structured as follows: narration which introduces and generalizes, dialogue scene of moderate length, narration, very short dialogue scene, closing paragraph of narration. "La última rubia" (*Cuentos malévolos*) has the following structure: introductory narration, short dialogue scene, narrative passage, short dialogue, narrative passage, short dialogue, closing narrative passage. Even in "El hombre del cigarrillo" where the dialogue is extensive, it is limited to one long scene in the middle specifically designed to underscore the theme of the narrative. Later writers are able to devote more space to dramatic scenes without sacrificing brevity by the use of an elliptical style which eliminates such details as dialogue lead-ins and encourages the reader to infer answers to questions. Palma limits the length and number of scenes rather than stripping their content.

As for order, the events in Palma's stories are in ordinary chronological sequence. There are no attempts to break the normal passage of time with brusque and illogical changes in the pattern of the narrative. Such experiments come later in the development of Peruvian fiction. In fact, the only chronological interruptions which Palma does allow are those purely expository passages which clarify, emphasize, or give a brief background for the incident.

Economy—the extent to which the author implies, rather than specifies—is also of fundamental importance to the brevity of the narrative. As has already been shown, Palma does not employ dialogue scenes as an economy measure. For all their restrictions, they are quite explicit. The material the reader must infer is found mostly between the lines of the expository passages. Descriptions of settings are kept to a bare minimum. The reader frequently meets the protagonists just as they are entering a "crossroads" experience, so that background information is naturally limited. With few exceptions, physical descriptions of the characters are brief or overlooked entirely. Another device which Palma employs in his longer stories is to divide the action into numbered sections. This technique provides much the same temporal advantage as is gained between the acts of a play. In other words, the author can make a time skip without accounting for the transitional details occurring between sections, and these can then be inferred by the reader. Such economy is in keeping with Palma's preoccupation with the single impression. The action must proceed rapidly forward to its climax and denouement. To do this, no specific detail may be included that does not tend to heighten the chosen impression.

The level of language usage, the idiomatic phrases and the embellishments which Palma has his narrators and characters employ, follows logically from the social and educational level of the people. There is, therefore, a notable lack of linguistic variety. Palma's characters represent a wide range of nationalities, but they are inevitably sophisticated, well-educated, ironically witty, and seemingly able to live comfortably without working very hard at a profession. They are given to esoteric literary and artistic pursuits, so it is not surprising that classical allusions should abound or that references to rare tapestries, manuscripts, and obscure bibliographical items should be made. Naturally, Palma does not need typographical indicators of local dialect such as misspellings and apostrophes. These devices become common later, when Peruvian fiction enters a more nationalistic phase.

Except for the occasional appearance of his stories in anthologies of Latin American fiction, Clemente Palma has been largely ignored outside of Peru. For that matter, his significant contribution to the history of Peruvian literature has gone relatively unnoticed in his own country. But the fact remains that he was instrumental both in giving the Peruvian fiction of the turn of the century a more universal orientation and in initiating the modern short story form. The content of most of his stories can generally be categorized as shocking and bizarre. However, far more important is their dominantly pessimistic and ironic tone which reveals a man sensitive to the spirit of his times and acutely aware of the special moral and spiritual problems of modern civilization. In this respect he forms a vital link with the post-World War II writers whose thematic obsession is the search for values in man and society.

# II

## NATIONAL SETTINGS
## AND CHARACTERS

THE NEXT PERIOD, a crucial one in the history of the Peruvian short story, begins just before World War I and extends into the early 1920's. It is during this time that national settings and characters are first used in the modern short story form. Abraham Valdelomar, Enrique López Albújar, and Ventura García Calderón, the principal writers responsible for this accomplishment, had actually begun their narrative production during the preceding period with works in the manner of Palma—not only studiedly cosmopolitan in background and character, but frequently given to decadent themes. That they again coincide in the more mature phase of their writing careers is of fundamental importance to the development of Peruvian fiction; their national stories mark the beginning of a dominant rural-regional trend which lasts until the fifties when moral questions and the problems of urban living become a preoccupation.

Given the distinct and unusual geographical zones of Peru, the national stories of Valdelomar, López Albújar, and García Calderón tend to group themselves conveniently according to coastal, sierra, or jungle settings. Though a short narrative necessarily limits background descriptions, the essence of each region is strikingly conveyed in their works. Valdelomar is particularly good with the Peruvian coast, that long, narrow strip of monotonous desert which forms such a sharp contrast with the colorful, constantly changing waters of the Pacific. López Albújar and García Calderón both capture the majestic, uncompromising quality of the sierra. García Calderón's stories of the jungle express the dynamic growth and luxuriant beauty of his tropical settings.

Coincident with the use of national landscapes is the predilection for such typical characters of rural Peru as the humble fisherman, the mulatto peon, the village priest, the feudalistic hacienda owner, the superstitious jungle native, and the stoical Andean Indian.[1] It soon becomes apparent in reading the narratives of these three authors that each has a special gift for portraying one of the personalities from this cast: Valdelomar for the coastal villager, López Albújar for the sierra Indian, and García Calderón for the colorful plantation owner.

Finally, it should be noted that the three writers differ somewhat in matters of style. Despite their emphasis on the national scene, Valdelomar and García Calderón never lose their concern for *modernista* refinements. López Albújar, on the other hand, breaks sharply with his previous *modernista* manner to develop a more vigorous and vernacular style. Together, however, the three authors give a vision of the Peruvian landscape and an insight into its native peoples not found in any previous fiction.

Abraham Valdelomar was born in the small coastal town of Ica on April 27, 1888. Shortly thereafter, his father moved the family to the port of Pisco, the background of Valdelomar's early childhood and, subsequently, of his most famous stories. These were years of uncertainty and privation which he recalls with special sensitivity:

The sixth child in the family, I was born some years after the war. My father was unemployed and had left for other parts in search of work. I must have been about six, and the oldest of my brothers

no more than eighteen. . . . I recall those days of my childhood
with fear and tenderness. Just imagine my poor mother, surrounded by six children, all of them just waking up to life and its
terrible problems. We stood united in the face of destiny, and, in
order to defend ourselves against it, we clung to each other the
more tightly. In later years, the bond was never broken, and I
believe that our closeness was simply the continuation of that
deep feeling which made us aware, during those unhappy days, of
the necessity to uphold one another while my mother, tired and
worn from her burden, silently wept for us, our future, and our
childhood which was so lacking in laughter and cheer.° ²

Valdelomar was not only proud of his heritage, but also
irresistibly drawn by his childhood environment. He recalls
with deep feeling the strength and wisdom of the villagers
who taught him to be stoic in the face of tragedy and to
respect the grandeur and beauty of his natural surroundings.

At the age of nine, he was sent to Lima to study at the
Colegio de Nuestra Señora de Guadalupe. During his student
years there, he began his literary career rather precociously by
publishing a little periodical called *La Idea Guadalupana* in
collaboration with Manuel Bedoya. In 1907 he left the
Colegio to enroll in the University of San Marcos. At the same
time he was active in journalism, his initial contributions being
cartoons and caricatures. The magazine *Aplausos y Silbidos*
published his first cartoon in the September, 1906, issue. Other
cartoons appeared in *Actualidades* during 1907. That same
year, he acquired a degree of notoriety working as a carica-
turist for *Monos y Monadas* and *Gil Blas*, literary and variety
magazines of the time.

In 1909 and 1910, Valdelomar's first poems were published
in the periodicals *Contemporáneos* and *Ilustración Peruana*.
The year 1910 also marks the starting point for his success as a
prose writer. A short story entitled "El suicidio de Richard
Tennyson" was published in the January and February issues

° For original Spanish passages, see pages 166 ff.

of *Variedades* [3] and, in April, a series of short prose sketches under the title "Con Argelina al viento" began in the newspaper *El Diario*.[4] These were quickly followed by two novelettes of decadent inspiration: *La ciudad muerta* and *La ciudad de los tísicos*, published in 1911 in *Ilustración Peruana* and *Variedades* respectively. "El beso de Evans," a short story also reflecting his *fin de siècle* tastes, appeared the same year in the literary review *Balnearios*.

Such extraordinary journalistic activity naturally interfered with his studies at the University. It did not, however, diminish his political interests; he became an enthusiastic member of the student group working on behalf of Guillermo Billinghurst for president of the republic. When Billinghurst was elected in 1912, Valdelomar was given a job as director of the official newspaper *El Peruano* in reward for his faithful support. In 1913 he was sent to Rome to serve in the Peruvian legation. During the short time he spent there, Valdelomar underwent a spiritual crisis first evidenced in nostalgic letters which speak of a profound homesickness for his native land.[5] The nature of his literary production also began to change. Whereas his previous efforts had been strongly influenced by the decadents, D'Annunzio in particular, his subsequent works were notably more original and mature and include his magnificent evocations of the Peruvian coast.

With the overthrow of Billinghurst in 1914, Valdelomar resigned his post and returned to Peru. He went to work immediately as a special writer for the newspaper *La Prensa,* continuing in that capacity until 1918. During these years, he wrote short stories, poetry, essays, and informal articles not only for *La Prensa* but for other Peruvian periodicals as well. In 1916 Valdelomar founded a literary magazine, *Colónida,* which lasted for only four issues. It served, however, as a rallying point for a group of young writers, many of them from the provinces, who, with Valdelomar as their leader, pledged themselves to revitalizing the style and content of the literature of the time.[6] During this period, Valdelomar's dress and poses became noticeably more exaggerated; he seemed to set out purposely to create a reputation as an eccentric. A monocle, walking stick, and outlandish attire made the "Conde de Lemos"—as he was fond of calling himself—a notorious figure around Lima.

In late 1918, with a renewed interest in politics, Valdelomar abandoned his extravagant dress and manners to go on a speaking tour of many of the towns and villages on the Peruvian coast. He was so encouraged by the warm reception he received that he set out again, in early 1919, to visit Arequipa, Cusco, and Moquegua. His political ambitions resulted in his election as a representative to the Central Regional Congress. On November 1, 1919, he traveled to Ayacucho to attend a session of the Congress and that evening was a special guest at a banquet given in the hotel. During the course of the meal, he stepped out of the banquet room and, in a freak accident, fell down the stairs, critically injuring himself. He died in the early morning hours of November 2.

Abraham Valdelomar's short story production was not extensive, but it was the genre in which he excelled and the one from which his literary fame derives. His first and best known collection, El caballero Carmelo, was published in 1918.[7] It consists of sixteen narratives which had originally appeared in local newspapers and magazines between 1910 and 1917. These stories can readily be divided into two groups —those dealing with the Peruvian seacoast, in which many autobiographical elements are present, and those of a fantastic or purely imaginative nature.

The coastal narratives, Valdelomar's most significant literary contribution, are characterized by intimate childhood recollections and a sensitive presentation of the tiny port of Pisco, its landscape and its inhabitants. The richness of the stories comes, in part, from his curious ambivalence toward the childhood world. Joy and serenity are invariably tinged with sadness, and nostalgia is tempered with fear. He describes the port of Pisco as a peaceful little village, with the simple, neat dwellings of fishermen scattered along its coastal sands. Valdelomar is especially drawn to these people because of their honest, uncomplicated response to life. He likes to picture the old men working in the warmth of the noonday sun, patiently mending the nets, while naked children cavort about. Despite their poverty, the young men and women are strong and proud and have achieved a certain harmony with their surroundings. This same tranquility and harmony is duplicated in their personal relationships.

Next to his boat sleeps a strapping young man of the sea. Lulled by the warmth of the breeze and the sand . . . his powerful, bare chest . . . rises and falls in time with the unsurpassed, God-given rhythm and harmony of the life that surrounds him. (pp. 16–17)

Their annals were never sullied by discord. They were a moral and austere people; a husband's lips kissed only those of his wife. And love between man and woman, that inexhaustible source of hate and slander, was for them as natural and pure as the water from their wells. (p. 17)

But these fond evocations have their sad and foreboding side. Peaceful, beautiful landscapes are counterbalanced by those which are barren and ominous: "Out in the desert the palm trees, seemingly terrified by the silent aridity of their surroundings, huddle together in small groups, like the travelers who cross it, and like men in the face of danger" (p. 15). Glorious sunrises which fill everyone with a love for life are contrasted with the haunting nightfalls when the sea sings threateningly. And that sea which provides the fishermen with their livelihood can also be their grave.

It is the implacable enemy of the people . . . particularly of the fishermen who venture out in their fragile boats, and of the wives who wait fearfully for their husbands' return at dusk. It is the implacable enemy of all who live on its shore; a terrible enemy . . . which at times can turn into a treacherous whirlpool, carrying unwary fishermen out to a fearful vortex, preventing them from ever returning to shore. (p. 55)

Valdelomar maintains this ambivalent tone even in his personal recollections of his homelife. The comforting warmth of the family circle is captured vividly in such passages as the following:

I used to wake up happily in Pisco. . . . In the radiant glow of the morning we used to hear mother's footsteps in the dining room as she prepared coffee for papa. . . . The crowing of our rooster was answered, at intervals, by all the other roosters in the area. . . . We could hear the roar of the ocean and smell the freshness of the morning. Afterwards, my mother would come to tend to us. She had us kneel by our beds, still dressed in our white night shirts, to say our prayers. (pp. 12–13)

However, the happiness and security of this picture contrasts with another typical scene: a stormy night with the father absent and the atmosphere charged with unspoken apprehension.

We ate without saying a word. Mama didn't eat anything. And in the silence of that sad night, I could see that she never took her eyes off the empty place which my father should have occupied. . . . The only thing to be heard was our silverware striking the plates, or the muffled steps of the servant, or the noise of the wind blowing through the trees in the garden. Mama spoke only twice in her sweet, sad voice:

"Son, don't eat that way with your spoon."

"Daughter, don't eat so fast." (p. 47)

In "Los Ojos de Judas," one of Valdelomar's most respected stories, this same feeling of mystery and foreboding dominates his portrayal of a boy's reactions to the somber events of Holy Week, which culminate in the burning of a frightening effigy of Judas. The surface events of the narrative are slight, involving little more than the child's very brief acquaintance with a lady whom he calls the "señora blanca" and her subsequent drowning on the night the effigy is burned. The author is primarily interested in creating an atmosphere whereby, without recourse to analysis, he can help the reader to sense the profound impact of these events on the boy's mind. He does this by deliberately obscuring the line of action. The boy's activities, particularly his acquaintance with the "señora blanca," have a hazy ambiguity. His reaction to familiar surroundings is filled with melancholy and foreboding. Valdelomar conveys this mood through a mystery-shrouded setting. The ocean, in particular, assumes a magical, subtly ominous role.

One meditates continually at the seashore. One is aware of the eternal ebb and flow of the tide, the ever present horizon, the ships that sail by in the distance, heading for unknown ports, the boats, lost in the heavy morning mist, sounding their horns frantically like lonely, lost souls seeking companionship in a world of shadows. (pp. 43–44)

The overwhelming solitude of the sea lurks behind every scene, always ready to interrupt and fill the mind with melancholy presentiments:

From the window of my bedroom I could look out on the garden and see a lonely and bedraggled grapevine which clutched and twined around some rusty old bars. Its leaves were withered from the effects of the salt air. Upon waking in the morning, I used to look out across the garden to the sea which could be seen in the background. Out there, ships sailed by, their tangled locks of lead-colored smoke dissipating in the blue sky. Other ships, accompanied by flocks of gulls which floated along beside like bits of foam, approached the port, growing larger and larger as they neared. Upon dropping anchor, they were immediately surrounded by swift little boats which gave the appearance of hungry ants attacking a dead insect. (p. 44)

The sea, and the things of the sea, are thus used to produce a sensation of melancholy and a premonition of tragedy. Even during a familiar walk along the beach, the boy suddenly feels himself alone—isolated, as it were, in time and space—lost in a world of mystery and *soledad:*

I walked for a long time and suddenly found myself in the middle of the path. To the north was the now distant port of Pisco which seemed to be enveloped in a shimmering vapor. The houses appeared small, and the pine trees were scarcely visible because of the distance. . . . The ships in the port had an abandoned air, as if they had been run aground by a hostile south wind. . . . In the midst of this lonely setting, I was gripped by a chilling sense of foreboding. I felt alone, isolated, seemingly lost on one of those remote and unknown stretches of beach where birds come to die. Then a wondrous silence fell over me; little by little the sound of the breakers was stilled, and I remained there motionless. . . . There was neither sight nor sound of life. Everything was silent and lifeless. (pp. 48–49)

The climax of the Holy Week celebration in the village and the crisis of the boy's fears occur simultaneously, at the burning of the Judas effigy. It is a stormy night, and while the fire blazes the two huge eyes of the effigy seem to gaze steadily and fiercely at the sea as if expecting some final tragedy. Suddenly shouts are heard in the distance indicating that a drowned person is being brought to shore. It is the "señora blanca." In life she had been shrouded in such mystery that she seemed but a figment of the boy's overexcited imagination, a symbol of his undefined presentiments. In death she becomes real, thus, suddenly, crystallizing all of the vague fears which had been haunting him.

Most of Valdelomar's evocations of childhood can be classified as stories of initiation or discovery in that they portray the progress of the protagonist from innocence to a knowledge of the nature of evil as it relates to his life and surroundings. In each situation, the boy becomes aware of human frailty, but is not quite able to cope with his new knowledge. And herein lies the charm of these works, for in them the boy's fears, hopes, disappointments, and confusions are made poignantly real as he faces problems and moral definitions which the more sophisticated adult mind takes for granted or rationalizes.

The title story of the collection, "El caballero Carmelo," compares favorably in depth of insight and symbolic richness with other more famous stories of initiation. It tells of a child's painful discovery of harshness and thoughtlessness in the adult world. The plot is simple. El caballero Carmelo, a venerable fighting cock has, over the years, become not only the pride of the family but a dearly loved pet as well. A young fighting cock has since been recognized as the champion of the village, and, in the face of boastful challenges by the new cock's owner, the father of the family feels obliged to bring the pet out of retirement to fight once more. The children plead with the father, but his pride is at stake and he refuses to listen to them. The old cock emerges victorious but badly wounded and dies within a few days, despite the youngsters' loving ministrations.

Almost from the beginning of the narrative, it is apparent that the boy is unconsciously establishing a comparison between animal life and human morality, with the old fighting cock the embodiment of the virtues he most admires. This admiration for the pet is cast in terms which are essentially human. For the lad, his cock is *"un hidalgo altivo, caballeroso,"* a champion of champions, who is at the same time just and prudent. Even more, he is a faithful friend who gives the family love and devotion. Thus, to the boy, the pride he sees in the adult world, more specifically his father's pride, seems incomprehensible when it would almost surely mean the death of such a pet. As the fight begins, the boy is further shocked by the callous attitude of the spectators who by their excited betting seem not to care that El caballero Carmelo might die. It causes him, unconsciously, to make a revealing comparison. Whereas Carmelo implicitly symbolizes that which is admirable in men, the young cock is seen to embody undesirable human traits: "To tell the truth, the other cock seemed anything but well-bred, and his actions were as insolent as they were human" (p. 20). Through this painful experience, the lad discovers that a man, even his own father, is capable of choosing what may bring sorrow. He also is forced to acknowledge that what affects him deeply may be of no concern to others. The result of this initiation is a necessary loss of innocence; a certain beauty and charm have gone out of life. And his loss of innocence—the realization that the high human ideals epitomized in El caballero Carmelo are not always attainable—is fittingly symbolized by the death of his pet.

A similar theme is developed in "El vuelo de cóndores" which tells of the visit of a circus to the town. One of the performers is a young girl who does a dangerous trapeze act. The crowd reacts so enthusiastically to her performance that the ringmaster orders her to give an encore during which she falls and is seriously hurt. The young narrator is at first thrilled by the exciting sights and sounds of the circus. Significantly, however, he does not enjoy the trapeze act and suffers through every moment of it. The crowd's insistence that she repeat the performance frightens and angers him, and when the girl falls as the result of the encore, he is filled with sadness and disgust: "Papa had us leave. We walked through the streets, caught the little bus, and I, sad and silent, with the shouts of the crowd still ringing in my ears, thought all manner of confused and bitter things against those people. For the first time in my life, I realized that there were very evil people in this world" (p. 31). Despite his last words, however, his shock does not come from the discovery that bad men and evil exist in the world. He understands that there are good people and wicked people. His discovery is more fundamental. As in the case of the previous story, he is initiated to the truth that selfish acts and attitudes can cause tragedy and suffering. He recognizes, ironically, what the audience fails or refuses to recognize: that they enjoy seeing a child's life in danger, and that this lust for excitement has contributed to her injury.

The use of first person narration is especially effective in both of these stories. The author is able to present the crucial action through the mind of a boy whose sensitivity colors the whole mood of the narrative. We come to know the boy by observing him and his reactions to the situation, rather than through any descriptions or analyses by the author. Thus, at the boy's moment of discovery, we too are awakened to the basic immorality of actions and events that adults accept without a second thought.

Although Valdelomar's purely imaginative narratives have neither the originality nor charm of his coastal tales, they are worth noting briefly, if only for contrast. "El beso de Evans" and "Fenix desolatrix," two works written early in his career, reflect a skeptical and pessimistic worldview clearly inspired by the same *fin de siècle* currents of decadence that influenced Palma. Bizarre humor is found in "El círculo de la muerte" and "Tres senas, dos ases," which were doubtless conceived during a brief stopover in New York in 1913 when Valdelomar was enroute to the Peruvian legation in Rome. These stories, called "Cuentos yanquis," deal in a tongue-in-cheek manner with wild get-rich-quick schemes and suicide plans. Valdelomar achieves his comic effects by caricature and a mock serious treatment of situations fraught with absurdity. Though these narratives exhibit little in the way of character insight, they do show a certain flair for the spirit of those crazily turbulent pre–World War I years in New York. They reveal, in fact, that same sensitivity to environment which he was able to exploit so effectively in his national stories.

*El caballero Carmelo* also includes five stories designated as "Cuentos chinos," all of which had been published previously in *La Prensa*. They represent Valdelomar's only bitterly satirical production, their sole purpose being to criticize Peruvian politics. These narratives, which purport to take place back in the times when Confucius taught classes in ethics at the University of Pekin, contain thinly veiled attacks

against the *hambrientos desalmados,* those greedy and inhuman politicians who make a mockery of honesty, and the *Pozo
Siniestro,* the members of Congress who fomented the upris-
ing against President Billinghurst, Valdelomar's benefactor.

The last of Valdelomar's varied short stories to be examined
are his so-called "Cuentos incaicos." One entitled "Chaymanta
Huayñuy," was included in *El caballero Carmelo,* but it
remained for Manuel Beltroy to make a complete collection of
these stories which were published in 1921 with the title *Los
hijos del sol.*[8] In these works, Valdelomar turns to pre-Colum-
bian Peru for inspiration. Some of the narratives are based on
well-known Inca legends; others are apparently original. But
in all, the author exploits the picturesque and the exotic in a
highly stylized, artificial manner. Whereas Valdelomar's man
of the coast is genuine, his sierra Indian is more properly a
fairy tale character. The hero of "El alfarero" is a good
example. He is an "inspired" artist who is willing to use his
own blood to achieve ideal blends of color and from his lips
come such unlikely speeches as: "I would like to capture in
one small piece all that my eyes behold. I long to encompass
nature itself, to do what the river does with the trees and the
heavens, to reproduce my natural surroundings as they are.
But I am not able to do so. I lack the formula for colors which
would express accurately what I feel in my soul" (p. 9).

The author occasionally strikes a markedly erotic tone—a
sharp contrast to the maternal and child love of his coastal
narratives. In the following quotation from "Chaymanta Huayñuy," passion rules:

She said to me: "Chasca, Chasca! Love me again, love me again,
just one more time. Even though you see fit, afterwards, to throw
my body into the river, or to abandon me here on the rocks where
the condors can feast on my flesh; although you take my scalp as
your trophy or make my skin the covering for your drums; even if
you use my teeth for your amulets, love me, love me again, love
me one more time!" . . . As she clung to my neck, hoarse,

inarticulate sounds came from her throat; her lips were burning and dry, and her eyes shone with a strange light. (p. 78)

Through exuberant use of adjectives, particularly those relating to color and emotion, short sentences with emphasis on the perfect tense, employment of Quechua words (not always accurately), and a conscious effort to create an atmosphere of mystery through such devices as timing the action at twilight, Valdelomar succeeds in creating stylistically and artistically unusual stories in this collection.

Valdelomar was a restless, active man who, in the thirty years of his life, had a wide variety of experiences as a politician, world traveler, journalist, and writer. He was also a complex personality, who, though adopting on occasion the pose of an eccentric, was, at the same time, capable of infinite tenderness. This versatility is reflected by his experiments with themes and forms. Satire, irony, bizarre humor, exoticism, and a rich variation in plot characterize his purely imaginative narratives. As for literary value and historical significance, however, the author's stories of the Peruvian coast are his most important. The genius of evocation and the sensitivity to character and surroundings give these tales an intrinsic value not found elsewhere in his production.

Enrique López Albújar was born in Chiclayo on November 23, 1872. When he was only six years old, he was sent to live with his grandparents in Piura.[9] His father and mother had moved to the isolated area of Morropón in hopes of improving their lot; but because it was dangerous and the schools were bad they did not take him with them. There can be little doubt that the move had much to do with shaping López Albújar's personality. Suddenly separated from the loving care of his parents, the boy was placed in an indifferent, even hostile environment. His grandmother, though well-meaning, was too preoccupied with other cares to give him much attention, and his aunt and cousins were often openly antagonistic. He recalls some of these experiences in a frank and charming little work entitled *De mi casona:*[10]

My grandmother paid little heed to me at first. One might even say that my presence made her a bit uncomfortable. And I can understand how she could possibly have felt that way. For a woman who was so devout in her Catholicism that she felt the need for confession during Lent, I could only be a continual reminder of her son's indiscretion. . . . As for my Aunt Isabel, she seemed not to have noticed that I was around. She looked at me out of the corner of her eye and addressed me in only the most indirect manner. Completely ignoring the fact that we were, after all, related, she was in the habit of making hateful distinctions which I, in my precociousness, understood only too well. These slights were added to my store of little sadnesses which, at times, caused me to weep silently in some out-of-the-way corner of that old house. (p. 27)

The experience made him independent, proud, and uncompromising, characteristics which he has displayed throughout his career as author and judge:

The way of life in that old house, where the activities were many and varied, but always impersonal, quickly taught me to take the initiative, to act independently, aggressively, and positively, despite the slights and insults which I suffered. I learned how to reply stingingly to the oblique comments which came my way, to do physical battle with my cousins when the occasion demanded it, and to return with pride the scornful glances of those around me. In a word, I learned to trust only in myself. (pp. 28–29)

López Albújar also gives a full account of his attempts to gain a primary education in the schools of Piura, introducing a wide variety of would-be teachers who might come straight from the pages of a picaresque novel. His first instructor was Maestro Piedra, a repulsive, foul-smelling man whose sadistic tendencies were exceeded only by his abysmal ignorance. He viewed his role primarily as that of warden and at every possible opportunity would make use of a whip which was kept near his desk. In general, what his teachers lacked in knowledge and teaching ability, they made up for in frequent and brutal disciplinary measures. In all of his schoolboy experiences in Piura, he met only one competent teacher, Germán Leguía, who, he states, gave him a fine foundation in grammar.

In 1886 López Albújar made his first trip to Lima to begin his secondary education. He is fond of relating how his writing career actually began at the tender age of fifteen when classmates discovered his poetic talents and called upon him to write tender verses of love to their sweethearts.

From 1891 to 1894 López Albújar combined studies toward a law degree at the University of San Marcos with politics, journalism, and some lively escapades. By that time his father was able to supply him with enough money to live comfortably, even ostentatiously. Always impeccably, often showily dressed, young López Albújar soon was a well-known and controversial figure about town. He engaged in many sports and was an accomplished fencer and boxer, skills which he admits stood him in good stead on more than one occasion.[11] His newspaper work was both literary and political, as, for the first time, he seriously turned to writing. The majority of these early pieces were published in *El Perú Ilustrado, El Progresista, La Integridad, La Cachiporra,* and *La Tunda,* short-lived newspapers and magazines of the time. Most of his initial works were poems, but it was a prose sketch—by present-day standards only mildly erotic—appearing in *La Tunda* that won him his first major notoriety, albeit under rather uncomfortable circumstances. The editor, in his eagerness to attract a wide reading public, appended the subtitle "Artículo que no debe leerse" to the sketch. Unfortunately, it thereby reached the attention of some oversensitive souls, including the district attorney, who were scandalized by what they termed its immoral content.[12] In May of 1893, he found himself in even worse difficulties because of his political writing. The work in question was a poem entitled "Ansias" that bitterly criticized the military despotism of General Cáceres.[13] The immediate result was forty days of imprisonment after which he faced a special type of trial known as a *Juicio de Imprenta.* Such famous men as Javier Prado and Pedro Labarthe composed the august tribunal that quickly found the fiery young López Albújar innocent.[14]

Between 1895 and 1899, López Albújar remained in Lima and continued to contribute articles to all the major newspapers and magazines of the city. His first book, *Miniaturas,* was published in 1895.[15] This cooperative effort with another young writer, Aurelio Arnao, contained twenty-three photoengravings of local beauties from the city's social register. Each picture was accompanied by a commentary in prose and verse which extolled the charms of the young lady in question. Needless to say, it was a bombshell in the ultra-conservative society of nineteenth-century Lima, and the wrath of fathers and fiancés was so aroused that López Albújar received three challenges to duels.

In 1904 López Albújar successfully passed his bar examination in Piura. During the following few years he practiced law, twice acted as a temporary judge, once as district attorney, and found time to teach a history course in the Colegio Nacional de San Miguel. He also continued his journalistic activities, founding and directing for three years a vigorous weekly entitled *El Amigo del Pueblo* in which he fearlessly attacked all types of social injustice.[16] In 1911, after a brief stay in Lima, he returned once again to Piura, assuming for a time the directorship of a daily newspaper *El Deber.* In July of 1916 he was called back to the capital by his close friend Augusto Durand to become chief editor of the large daily newspaper *La Prensa.* He remained there for just six months and then received an appointment as judge in Huánuco. Taking this post was, he believes, a major turning point in his life. For it was there, in the Peruvian sierra, that he was able for the first time to observe the Indian carefully in his own environment and subsequently to write about him with such conviction.

Just being there, however, did not lead automatically to writing the famous *Cuentos andinos* in which he masterfully places the Indians of the sierra within the framework of the modern short story. This work was directly due to an unpleasant incident associated with his duties as judge. Faced with a choice between rendering a decision which would please his superiors or following the counsels of his own conscience, he chose the latter course. For that decision he received a severe reprimand from a higher court and was suspended for three months. He and his wife retired to a hacienda in the area where he wrote his masterpiece. Readily admitting that *Cuentos andinos* might never have been conceived except for that humiliating episode, he points to it as an example of how even the most unpleasant experiences of life are sometimes blessings in disguise.

In 1923 López Albújar settled again in Piura where he wrote his most famous novel, *Matalaché*. In 1929 he was appointed temporary judge in Chiclayo and in 1930 he returned to Lima to take over the government post of Director of Cultural Education. The August revolution of that year cut short the appointment, and in 1931 he went to Tacna as judge of the Superior Court. He made his home for more than twenty years in that city, spending much of his time writing. Several of his most significant works were: *Los caballeros del delito* (1936), a sociological study of banditry; *El hechizo de Tomayquichua* (1943), a novel; *Nuevos cuentos andinos* (1937), short stories; and *De la tierra brava* (1938), poems. He also wrote many of his as yet unpublished works at this time. López Albújar eventually rose to the presidency of the Superior Court of Tacna, holding the position with dignity and honor until his retirement at the age of seventy-five.[17] Afterwards he took up residency again in Lima where he has remained an active figure.

His short story production actually begins in the very last years of the nineteenth century with some of his first works being published in the daily *El Comercio* between 1897 and 1900. These stories plus others, which were also written during that period but which have never appeared in print, are contained in an unpublished manuscript entitled "La mujer Diógenes, cuentos de mi juventud." [18] Although they were written more than two decades before his masterpiece, *Cuentos andinos,* they reveal the author's distinctive talent for character depiction. On the other hand, they give no hint of the vigorous and vernacular style which characterizes his narratives of the Peruvian sierra. These works of his youth are after the manner of Clemente Palma, studiedly cosmopolitan, and reflect the obvious influence of the decadents. Skepticism, irony, refined perversity, pseudo-scientific ostentation, and fantasy are the essential ingredients of these stylistically elegant, early stories.

"La mujer Diógenes," title story of the collection, tells of a rich young lady's attempts to find the perfect lover through the aid of a supernaturally endowed mesmerist. "El doctor Navá" deals with a deluded doctor's genetic theory for producing genius by scientific mate selection. "La gran payasada" treats of a man's revenge on high society by forcing people he despises to perform degrading acts in public. Finally, "Una frase" tells, with marked irony, of a young man who has great faith in the fidelity of his betrothed until he is rudely made aware of her cynicism and wickedness.

López Albújar continues in much the same style in a second unpublished manuscript entitled "Cuentos de arena y sol." [19] These stories, with the exception of two, were written between 1901 and 1916; most of them are dated 1915 and 1916. From the manuscript's somewhat misleading title, it could be assumed that the Peruvian seacoast forms the background for the narratives.[20] In reality, only two have national settings. The remainder of the collection is notably cosmopolitan, bearing strong resemblance to the earlier "La Mujer Diógenes: cuentos de mi juventud." The two exceptions, "El eterno expoliado" and "Una expresión de agravios," significantly foreshadow López Albújar's swing to a more vernacular style and the adoption of national settings and characters. The first work, published in his own weekly, *El Amigo del Pueblo,* is particularly noteworthy because of its didactic intent. It sympathetically relates the plight of an Indian who must pay unjust debts to a cruel hacienda owner and the corrupt clergy. Social protest is the main motive; however, it should be noted that it is the only work where the author shows more than an objective, literary interest in the Indian and his problems.

López Albújar's real significance in the history of the Peruvian short story and his international fame as a writer derive from *Cuentos andinos* (1920), a collection of ten narratives dealing with the sierra and its people.[21] The work can be said to represent a second phase in his narrative production since it reveals none of the *fin de siècle* tendencies which characterized his earlier fiction. There are occasional flashes of irony and humorous understatement, but, basically, the author is concerned with giving an authentic, sober portrayal of setting and character. Six of the narratives deal specifically with Andean Indians. López Albújar's understanding of their customs and their mentality is not as complete or as intimate as that of later writers, such as Ciro Alegría and José María Arguedas. His observations are limited to a few characteristics which especially impressed him. On the other hand, he succeeds in giving individuality to the native character, a fact which cannot be overemphasized since this is the first time in Peruvian fiction that the Indian appears as something more than a picturesque or curious stereotype. He becomes a flesh and blood person who has some of the same shortcomings and feels some of the same emotions as the reader.

Coincident with the individualization of the sierra Indians

is the author's objective approach to their situation. Despite the desire of some literary critics and historians to place him in the role of vindicator, he, in fact, has neither a socioeconomic ax to grind nor a particular interest in arousing sympathy for the Indian. He only seeks to show them in a more realistic light. It is almost a relief to see the all-too-familiar masks of the cowering, whimpering victim or the legendary noble savage stripped away and find that the Indian, while certainly an unsophisticated and even primitive character, has unsuspected introspective depths. López Albújar reveals that this native of the sierra can be a man of great tenacity who unwaveringly pursues a given course, though this trait may be disguised by his ability to dissimulate his motives before his own people as well as the white man. His fatal resignation to the pain, sorrows, and trials of life, which takes the form of an almost dumb impassivity, frequently conceals a curious, bright mind with a surprising capacity to learn and assimilate. It can also keep one from recognizing his sensitive appreciation of irony and his subtle, picaresque humor. And, finally, the Indian's timidity and seeming humility may blur the fact that he can be unswerving in his sense of justice, implacable in his hatred, and perverse in his cruelty.

Nowhere is the Indian's sly sense of humor better presented than in "La mula de taita Ramun" which deals primarily with the interesting relationship between the village priest and his humble parishioners. The narrative abounds in verbal irony such as is found in the following passage in which an Indian is protesting, in his own way, the high cost of a special mass: "*Taita*, you are taking my whole harvest away from me. It is for that very reason that Niceta was saying to me the other day, 'Listen, Marcelo, don't you think it would be a good idea for our Benito to study to be a priest?' 'What for?' I said. And she answered . . . 'Why, so he can work less and earn more like *taita* Ramun does.' " [22]

However, one of the facets of Indian character which most

fascinated the author, and not surprisingly so, is his sense of justice. "El campeón de la muerte," one of the author's most respected stories because of its technical excellence and dramatic force, demonstrates how vengeance and justice can fuse inextricably in the mind of the sierra Indian. The result is a deeply ingrained eye-for-an-eye retaliatory concept whereby the victim of a wrong is expected to seek revenge in a way which will correspond fittingly to the hurt he has suffered; the scales of justice will not be balanced until he accomplishes this end. The trait is particularly apparent in this narrative where the conflict is on a personal, man-to-man level. Liberato Tucto, the seeker of vengeance, is an aged, feeble man whose daughter has been brutally murdered. His physical debility, however, is compensated for by his patience and cunning. He bides his time until he is able to enlist the aid of the accomplice who is most likely to extract an appropriate revenge—not just a simple killing, but a slow, painful death. Hilario Crispín, the object of vengeance, is a worthy antagonist whose cruelty is exceeded only by his cynicism and guile. As if to save the trouble of an investigation, he arrogantly dumps the desecrated remains of the daughter at Tucto's feet. He is both resigned to the fact that he must now act as quarry and confident of his ability to survive in his remote mountain refuge. Juan Jorge, the instrument of revenge, is a deadly rifle shot, a sort of gunman-for-hire, who kills for the sake of justice, although the money and the thrill of pitting his skill against that of another make his job more exciting. Because of the nature of the crime and the high bounty offered, he agrees to riddle Crispín with ten shots, but not to put him out of his misery until the tenth one. Despite different motives, the characters are much alike in their capacity for calculated brutality. Patiently, fatalistically, each plays out his role. Tension mounts steadily until the climax when Crispín is killed in the prescribed manner, and the balance of justice is properly restored.

The power of the narrative clearly lies in the convincing presentation of unusual characters. First of all, they are psychologically credible; despite their unusual capacity for hatred and cruelty, they express basic human drives and instincts. Furthermore, they follow a logical pattern within the story. That is, the character is always consistent with his action. To rapidly and convincingly establish a character as a real person within the limited framework of a short story is, of course, a subtle matter, and López Albújar's skill in this respect is worth noting. The psychological portraitures are delineated through every action of the story so that at the climax his protagonists are both complete and persuasive. His most obvious and effective technique for establishing the essential facets of all three personalities is the recording of their reactions to events. Tucto's reaction to the sight of his daughter's body, Juan Jorge's reaction to the first sight of his quarry, and Crispín's reaction after being discovered reveal each character's fundamental traits with such clarity that no author analysis is necessary. One of the most notable examples of this technique is seen in the encounter between Crispín and Tucto at the beginning of the narrative:

"Old man, here's your daughter. Now you won't have to go around looking for her any longer. . . ." And without waiting for a reply, the man, who was none other than Hilario Crispín, opened the sack and dumped its sickening contents out on the ground. . . . It was, indeed, Tucto's daughter. . . . But the old man . . . exclaimed:
"You better take the sack with you; it's probably stolen and would bring me nothing but bad luck. But since you have brought back my daughter, you ought to give me something so I can buy candles for the wake and provide for those who will come to it. Have you got a *sol* on you by chance?" (pp. 35–36)

In López Albújar's stories of the Andean Indians, the conflict is usually only an outer conflict—between one character and another. This limitation, of course, does not prevent him from producing works of great sensitivity and penetration in which the protagonists reveal much about themselves while acting out the conflict. Occasionally, however, the author adds another dimension by also depicting a character's struggle within himself. Such is the case in "El licenciado Aponte" which tells of the return of an Indian to his home after military service. At the same time, there is an important sociological question here because both the community and personal problems which can arise from such a situation are sometimes tragic. A conscript is usually sent to the coast immediately after induction. In this strange environment he has to adjust to new ideas which are often contrary to his tradition. The return home, however, often proves to be even more difficult, for he may innocently cause serious family and community ruptures over new standards versus old beliefs.

Juan Maille, the hero of this story, is unable to reconcile his new knowledge with the traditions of the community. In a sense, the military experience may be said to have produced in him a loss of the innocence which was essential to his old way of life. His former ideas of authority and ritual are undermined, and he sees that new methods are sometimes superior to ways which had seemed tried and true. He also learns some very practical skills, such as how to read, handle a gun, and live by his wits under varying circumstances. Despite his greatly broadened vision of life and his expanded self-knowledge, the memory of the sierra remains strong, and he longs to return.

The joy of coming home, however, proves illusory precisely because of his altered sense of values. The community's way of life now seems strangely out of step. For the other inhabitants of the community who do not trust the "new" Maille, the feeling is mutual. As a result of the conflict, which each day grows more bitter, Maille abandons the area and gravitates to the life of an outlaw. At this point, the author focuses specifically on the protagonist's inner struggle. He feels himself a man without a country, suspended in time without a firm relationship to either past or present. The combination of environment and ingrained tradition continually draws him back to his old ways. His new vision of life, however, never quite allows the link with the past to be reforged. This inner conflict, only resolved in death, gives him a sense of lost continuity and, at the same time, an insecurity about the present where new values and beliefs have not been thoroughly established.

The authentic and forceful presentation of the Peruvian sierra and its Indians is continued in *Nuevos cuentos andinos,* composed by López Albújar during his tenure as judge in Tacna and published in Chile in 1937.[23] In general, he uses the same themes. The Indian's determination to seek a form of justice through revenge, for example, is found in "Cómo se hizo Pistaco Calixto." Its basic plot elements are very similar to "El campeón de la muerte," as again a young girl is abducted by a renegade Indian. The abductor is subjected to a relentless tracking by the girl's brother and eventually dies under his deadly gunfire. The study of the Indian who returns from military service is continued with some variation in "El brindis de los yayas." Whereas Maille's new ideas brought personal tragedy, Ponciano is able to make good use of his. Although his attempts to introduce innovations result in a serious cleavage in the community, the narrative ends on a more optimistic note. Again in these stories, López Albújar's purpose is not merely to arouse sympathy for his characters. He is concerned with portraying certain characteristics which interest him, and in so doing, he objectively depicts both their admirable and their less edifying qualities. If he fails to duplicate the genius of *Cuentos andinos,* it is because the books are so similar.

The last phase of López Albújar's short story production is represented by *Las caridades de la señora de Tordoya,* published in 1955.[24] This collection marks at least a partial return to the past, as, in a number of the narratives which have urban settings and characters, the author shows an affinity for themes reminiscent of his first short stories. Several of them can be compared to specific stories from his earlier collections, though the works of the last phase show the hand of an experienced writer. The same sophisticated and indulgent irony of "La mujer Diógenes" is found in "Las caridades de la señora de Tordoya," title story of the book. In both stories the heroine is a lovely and vain woman whom the author satirizes. "El delator," whose main character tries to predict human behavior through fingerprint types, bears a strong resemblance to "El doctor Navá" in its pseudo-scientific content. Finally, "Los esposos Diez," in which a husband forces his unfaithful wife to enslave herself to a vice, is similar in its skepticism and refined perversity to "La gran payasada." [25]

López Albújar's versatility makes him a successful writer of stories with varied theme and style. But, as in the case of Valdelomar, his national short stories are his most important contribution, both literarily and historically. His works of the sierra are one of the most significant developments in Indianist literature in Peru.

Ventura García Calderón was born in Paris on February 23, 1886, not long after the War of the Pacific between Peru and Chile (1879–83) in which Peru lost two provinces. His father, Francisco García Calderón, was President of the republic during this disastrous conflict. Because of his refusal to sign what he considered an unjust treaty, he was exiled and denied the right to return to Peru. The family moved about considerably, finally settling in Paris. A few months after García Calderón's birth, some members of the family were permitted to return to Peru, and he accompanied them. He remained there throughout childhood and early adulthood, and was graduated from the University of San Marcos.

In 1906 García Calderón traveled to France and began to

dedicate himself seriously to writing and journalism. In 1911 he was named chancellor of the Peruvian consulate in Paris; this was the beginning of a long career as a diplomat which he was able to combine successfully with his career as a writer. He later resigned this post for political reasons, but in 1913 he resumed his diplomatic duties, this time as Secretary of the legation in Spain. In 1916 he was sent to Le Havre as Consul, a post which he held until 1919, when he again resigned for political reasons. It should be noted here that during World War I García Calderón stood firmly on the side of the Allies and published a number of pro-Ally articles, particularly in the newspapers of Spain and Belgium.

In 1921 he returned again to diplomacy and for a short time was chief of the Peruvian propaganda office in Paris. During the course of this year, due to a political change in Peru, he began his longest absence from the diplomatic arena. He remained in Paris and dedicated his full time to a series of writing projects ranging from newspaper and magazine articles to serious linguistic and literary studies which were to bring him renown in the academic world. In 1930 García Calderón was asked to join the Peruvian legation in Belgium, and, after two years, he was sent to Brazil in a similar capacity. In 1933 he returned to Belgium to serve as a delegate to the League of Nations.

The eve of World War II found him as Minister Plenipotentiary in Belgium, and once again he embraced the Allied cause. *Cette France que nous aimons,* a book inspired by the German occupation of his beloved Paris, was written during this period.[26] Following World War II, García Calderón was appointed permanent delegate to UNESCO in Paris. He was active as a member of the executive council of that organization until his death on October 28, 1959. It is interesting to note that after leaving Peru in 1906, he had returned to his native land only twice—once in 1911 and again in 1949—for brief visits.

García Calderón's literary production is varied and vast. His work includes poetry, short stories, plays, essays, novels, literary and linguistic research, and innumerable articles of a less formal nature contributed to leading newspapers and magazines of Europe and Latin America. He was director of a number of journals including *La Revista de América, La Revue de L'Amerique Latine, América Latina,* and *La Revue Latine.* Among his most famous scholarly works are: *Del Romanticismo al Modernismo; Rubén Darío, pages choises; El nuevo idioma castellano; Semblanzas de América;* and *La vida del Buscón.* One of his most helpful contributions as far as his native country is concerned, is the twelve volume *Biblioteca de Cultura Peruana* which he compiled. This collection, which appeared in 1938, was financed by the Peruvian government and published by Desclée de Brouwer in Paris.

García Calderón was able to write in both Spanish and French with complete mastery.[27] So well was his work received in France that in 1933 a strong movement headed by such French celebrities as Louis Barthou, André Tardieu, Eduardo Herriot, Jacques Bainville, Gabriel Boissy, and Max Daireaux promoted him—without final success—for the Nobel Prize. Following the lead of France, a similar movement took place in Peru. In 1939, in an extraordinary demonstration of the respect with which he was regarded in the intellectual circles of Europe, he was received as a member of the Belgian Royal Academy; and in 1947 in *Hommage a Ventura García Calderón,* published in Paris, outstanding European authors and critics showed their admiration for him. In May of 1959 shortly before his death, he was honored by the French Civic Merit League for his contributions to culture.

The initial phase of García Calderón's short story production is represented by *Dolorosa y desnuda realidad* (1914), a collection of seventeen narratives which were written in 1910. Skepticism and irony pervade these works in which sadistic, unhappy women and worldly, disenchanted men feverishly

strive for unattainable goals and desires. Sir Robert, the
cynical and dissipated hero of "La domadora," turns to
perversion in a frantic effort to satisfy his lust. "La otra" tells
of Ricardo Gaul's insane desire to see his former mistress
reincarnated. Nymphomania is the subject of "La esclava."
The themes of these stories, which have little originality,
reflect the obvious influence of the French decadents. Their
technical excellence, on the other hand, is noteworthy.

The next, and most important, phase of García Calderón's
short story production begins with *La venganza del cóndor*
(1924), in which he turns to Peruvian settings and characters.[29] Like Valdelomar, who began to evoke childhood scenes
of his native Peru during his stay in Rome, García Calderón
also relies on memory mixed with liberal doses of imagination
in producing his narratives while in Europe. Despite his long
absence from Peru, he had ample personal experience on
which to draw. Shortly before making his definitive move to
France in 1906, he had taken an extended journey on
muleback into the rugged coastal and sierra terrain of Ancash
with the hope of staking a rich mining claim. His experiences
during that trip doubtless served as bases for a number of his
national narratives; and the device of having an inexperienced
young traveler narrate some of the stories adds an unmistakable autobiographical note to the collection. A necessary
insight into this collection as well as others of García Calderón's stories about Peru can be gained by recognizing that
the author is addressing his narratives essentially to a European audience. *La venganza del cóndor* was translated into a
number of languages and achieved immediate critical acclaim,
especially in France. Some of his national stories were written
first in French and only later translated into Spanish. Those
critics who, while reluctantly conceding his great talent, have
been so quick to attack García Calderón as *afrancesado*
because he failed to present the Indians and their socioeconomic conditions with sufficient authenticity or because his

works are not designed to protest, moralize, or make a serious study of native customs, would do well to consider his aims. He was concerned primarily with capturing, in fictional form, those highly unusual characteristics of his native country which have a basis in reality and, at the same time, a special appeal for foreign readers. Furthermore, García Calderón's pride in Peru and his Peruvian heritage comes through clearly in the way he personally associates himself with the national traits he is writing about and makes frequent references to "my country" and "my people."

It is obvious, of course, in his stories of the sierra that García Calderón had only a superficial knowledge of the Andean Indian, although we might also point out that most writers of Indianist fiction, including those concerned with social protest, have betrayed a woeful ignorance about this people. Unlike López Albújar, who is able to establish the sierra Indians as individuals whose traits and feelings have human significance, García Calderón portrays them only as representative types of a picturesque culture. He enjoys focusing on such fascinating characters as the village witch doctor or the *despenador* whose profession is to put slowly dying people out of their misery. He depicts even the more commonplace people as they participate in activities and rites which seem strange and exotic to the uninitiated. The colorful coca-chewing Indian, the Indian with a special attachment for the llama, the inscrutable Indian whose ways are beyond the ken of the white man, are unusual, but faceless, characters in his stories of the sierra.

At the same time, García Calderón—his critics notwithstanding—was aware of and sensitive to the contemporary Andean Indian's plight. To be sure, none of his stories is specifically designed to point up this plight; however, implications are made which clearly reveal his attitude. "La postrer amiga," for example, gives a moving portrayal of a sick old Indian whose only son has been taken from him to serve in the army.

Though he has been left without anyone to provide for his physical needs, his plea for help is rudely ignored by government officials and the church. Isolated passages sprinkled throughout García Calderón's narratives refer to the Indians as a long-suffering and oppressed people. Although García Calderón is mainly interested in creating stories which are fascinating, artistically excellent, and universal in appeal, he most certainly is not insensitive to the problems of the indigenous inhabitants of the sierra.

Those Andean tales of García Calderón which have a markedly autobiographical tone also, interestingly enough, belong to that type known as the story of initiation or recognition. The painful progress from innocence to knowledge is made in each case by a well-educated young Limeñan who enters the world of the Peruvian highlands for the first time. Although the exact terms of the initiation vary according to plot development, the discovery is basically the same in each story: The sierra and the value systems of its people are entirely different from anything the hero has known and his prejudices must be altered. A well-recognized aspect of every story of initiation is the hero's adjustment to his new-found knowledge. The more discerning the character, of course, the more sophisticated and complete is his reaction to the dilemma of adjustment. His first step is to recognize that there is a problem, and second, he must realize that the problem may have only a very limited solution.[30] His ability to live with the solution, no matter how unsatisfactory it may be, is the crucial stage in his understanding of himself and the new problem of existence which he has encountered.

While not one of García Calderón's best stories, "Juventud" is an excellent example of a hero's recognition and adjustment to the dilemmas found in a strange, new environment. The setting is a *tambo*, one of those humble way stations on a lonely mountain road designed for the traveler who is too tired to be particular about the comfort and cleanliness of his night's lodging. The hero, a young, inexperienced lawyer full of confidence in the law and the "civilized" approach to all matters, begins his painful initiation by losing a pair of boots to what had seemed to be a friendly fellow traveler. His predicament becomes more serious when he discovers that his pack mule is lame and that he is stranded unless someone supplies him with another animal. Unfortunately, his distress arouses little sympathy among the other travelers. A man who has several extra mules refuses to help the young "doctor," as he is branded by local inhabitants, preferring to tease him about his foolish "city ways." Finally, in a fit of frustration and rage, the young man pulls his gun on the tormentor and takes the mule he needs. He is immediately horrified, however, at having done such a thing: "It was at that precise moment that the young greenhorn burst into tears of rage and shame. Could it be possible that he, of all people, had committed that crime, that injustice? To which conquistador among his ancestors did he owe this sudden lapse into brutality?" [31]

His discovery and adjustment are not complete as yet, and he goes his way, hopefully repeating the articles of the *Código Civil* which he carries in his saddle bags next to his diploma. His next encounter is with a group of three Indians, two men and a woman. The woman is tied at the foot of a cross, and one of the men is beating her. The young man, who had read *Don Quixote* and whose heart throbs with such a glow of magnanimity that he feels capable of settling all of the world's problems, rushes in and frees the victim. The girl promptly spits in his face, telling him that her husband was only expressing his love. The literary allusion to Don Quixote is all too obvious. García Calderón has led his hero into complete disillusionment, and the adjustment which had begun earlier when he took the mule he needed by force is further advanced by his final act: "Then he took from his belongings the small copy of the Napoleonic Code and, going to the edge of the road, threw it, along with a whole bundle of civilized ideas and worthless illusions, into the condors' ravine" (p. 323).

In "La venganza del cóndor" and "Un soñador," the discovery and adjustment are presented in more subtle terms, but the theme is still the same. The inexperienced man of the city learns that his concepts and values have to be modified if he is to survive in his vast and demanding new environment. Nothing in his background has prepared him for the encounter, and the adjustment comes only as he learns from his unexpected and sometimes bitter experiences. The theme is one that, in a sense, is related to a subtle but persistent idea in the author's tales of the *selva* in which the ways of the white man and the jungle Indian are contrasted. The conclusion is always the same: The highly civilized man, for all his learning and technical progress, is not equipped to deal with the exotic and treacherous jungle environment. In "Las hormigas rojas," for example, the Indian character, after his encounter with white men, concludes, as does the reader, that "the witch doctors of the Sensi tribe know more about the mysteries of earth and heaven than do the foreign devils who have beards like monkeys and cover themselves like women" (p. 159).

In "Historias de caníbales" García Calderón goes a step further by establishing a direct and ironic comparison between European civilization and the so-called barbarism of the jungle native. The tone is humorous and only lightly mocking, but the implications are clear. The story concerns the visit of a famous French explorer to the Peruvian *selva*. He captures a young Indian maiden from a cannibal tribe and subsequently marries her. They remain in Peru for awhile and she quickly learns Spanish, her favorite words being those meaning "filthy," "liars," and "thieves," which, as the author is careful to point out, pretty well summed up civilization as far as she was concerned. Later she accompanies her husband to Paris, and her education begins in earnest when she enters the "jungle" of high society. After her husband's death, she returns to her tribe which hates her because she has been infected by the pernicious ways of modern civilization: "That is to say, she has learned to lie and to seduce the husbands of the other women. Furthermore, she refuses to bathe, as her companions do, in the sacred rivers of my homeland" (p. 388). García Calderón could scarcely be described as a romantic who calls the white man to the Arcadia of the Noble Savage. In fact, such stories as "La selva que llora," "Una mona," and "La selva de los venenos" show the jungle, for all its lush beauty, to be a place of hidden dangers. The ironic juxtaposing of modern man and primitive environment and society, however, reveals not only censure of modern civilization, but also the author's personal pride in the unusual aspects of his native country.

It is interesting to note that consciously or unconsciously this pride has led García Calderón to idealize the Indian girls of the sierra. In "El feto de vicuña," the narrator describes one as follows:

She was a splendid creature, born as it were of a summer night's dream! If ethnographers did not swear that this race had its origin in the high plateaus of Asia or the islands of the Pacific, we might well believe that they were straight out of the paintings of Renaissance or primitive Italian artists. Those tender, shining eyes, that skin gilded by the reflections of the snow. (p. 255)

The Indian girl described here proves that her character matches her physical beauty when she saves the life of the narrator at the risk of her own. In "Amor indígena," an Indian girl is similarly described: "The young girl's admirable breasts were clearly outlined under her strange mantle . . . and her delicate, dust-covered feet, in their coarse sandals, had a certain Biblical charm" (p. 50). Her faithfulness, even in the face of cruelty, causes the narrator to ask: "Who else would love me so faithfully that she would follow in my horse's hoofprints in search of her loved one as in the sublime *Song of Songs?* What other girl would pursue me, disheveled, forsaking her own and surrendering herself to me for life (p. 55)?"

If the idealized Indian girl does not by implication outshine her more civilized white counterpart, she at least stands out as an excellent example of womanhood. Once again in assessing García Calderón's intent, it is helpful to recall that, as a Peruvian in Europe, he is addressing his national narratives essentially to a foreign audience. It is not unnatural that he should idealize what is most charming and primitive in his native land.

Most notable in García Calderón's coastal narratives are the heroes, who are fitting descendants of the Spanish *conquistadores*. Fierce fighters, implacable enemies, punctilious in the adherence to their idea of honor, these characters seem almost to have been transplanted from a Calderonian *comedia* to a rural American setting where the conditions are different but the code is just the same. In "Corrida de gallos," the heroes, Fulgencio Fabres and Tadeo Santiván, are two of the richest and most feared men in the province, whose pride and honor are at stake in a symbolic battle between their prize fighting cocks. Though the two men follow all the time-honored rules of decorum in a manner befitting dignified *hidalgos,* their smouldering antagonism and the deeper significance of the cock fight are not lost on the humble onlookers. When Fabres' cock flees from his adversary in apparent confusion and fear rather than fight to the death, the owner reacts in the only way his code will permit. He shoots his own cock and challenges Santiván to a personal duel. "Murió en su ley" presents the classic challenge to the *hidalgo's* code of honor: the unfaithful wife caught with her lover. To no one's surprise, Jenaro Montalván, the irate husband, brutally murders his errant spouse and then devotes the rest of his life to the pursuit of the "other man" in order to avenge the blot on his name. "El alfiler" is similar in theme. The main character prefers to see his beloved daughter killed rather than to overlook her unfaithfulness to the son-in-law. The aura of "invincibility" surrounding these twentieth-century characters, who seem to have their roots in another more violent and demanding era, is graphically depicted in "En los cañaverales." The hero is a young plantation owner who tries to live up to the reputation of his father, Crisanto Samanés, who is respected and loved like a Latin American Cid. The hero has been repeatedly humiliated by a neighbor and is losing the respect of his peons until, at one bold stroke, he kills the neighbor and burns his cane fields, thus proving himself a worthy successor to his father.

Heroines play an outstanding role in his other coastal stories. Again, the characters seem to have been transported by the author from another environment into the rural Peruvian setting. Impressive in their evil beauty, they are perfect examples of the *femme fatale* of decadent fiction and reminiscent of García Calderón's other heroines from *Dolorosa y desnuda realidad* who committed their diabolical acts in the more artificial environs of Paris and London. All the essentially evil characteristics of the *femme fatale* are present in the heroines of "Chamico" and "Filomena," who are able, it seems, to rise to new heights of cruelty in their rural surroundings.

Following *La venganza del cóndor*, García Calderón published four more collections in Paris (all in French) which are, in a sense, continuations of that masterpiece. Again Peru's distinctive geographical regions form the setting. *Danger de mort*, containing twenty-two tales, appeared in 1926. This work was followed in 1927 by a less important book, *Si Loti était venu*, consisting of a novelette and three short stories. *Couleur de sang*, which appeared in 1931, contains twenty short narratives. Finally, in 1936, the author published *Le sang plus vite*, containing a fine selection of stories which had appeared in his earlier works, plus a few which were new.

Other short story collections published by García Calderón —*Virages* (1933) and *Le serpent couvert de regards* (1947)— do not have Peru as a background. As in his first book of stories, they present characters and settings which are European. It is interesting to note that most of these narratives were subsequently translated into Spanish, many by the author himself.

As has been indicated, García Calderón's short stories include both national and cosmopolitan narratives. As in the case of Valdelomar and López Albújar, his Peruvian works are artistically and historically the most significant. Admittedly, he did not have the gift that his two contemporaries had for depicting national characters. This should not, however, detract from the reader's appreciation of García Calderón's pride in Peru and his unusual skill as a storyteller.

As for the technical aspects of their short story production, Valdelomar, López Albújar, and García Calderón follow generally in the steps of Clemente Palma, especially in the fundamental consideration of single effect or impression. Nothing need be said, therefore, concerning such technical matters as the ordering of events in these works. And as for the narrative point of view, we need only mention that unlike Palma, who wrote mostly in the first person, Valdelomar, López Albújar, and García Calderón did not confine themselves so exclusively to one point of view. As a matter of fact, all of the various types of focus can be found in their stories: first-person, first-person observer, author-observer, and omniscient author.

Regarding the use of particularized or dramatic scenes and the use of generalization, the three authors follow a procedure which is also closely akin to that of Clemente Palma: the interspersing of a limited number of dialogues—which have the effect of dramatic scenes—with narrative passages. As in the case of Palma's dialogues, the speeches are coherent and detailed, and the limitation of the number and length of these dramatic scenes serves the interests of brevity. A basic difference, however, can be seen in the nature of the dramatic passages of Valdelomar's and López Albújar's works where characterization assumes a greater importance. Both of those authors see more clearly than either Palma or García Calderón the possibility of dialogue scenes having an important or even major part in portraying character. Valdelomar's dramatic family scenes in the humble coastal home give insights into the personality of a boy and his relationship to his family which need not be augmented by external analysis. In a similar manner, López Albújar designs the conversations among the Indians to help us see them as individuals.

In the style of the dialogue—the idiomatic phrases and embellishments with which Valdelomar, López Albújar, and García Calderón provide their speakers—there is a significant variation from Palma's usage. Because of their subject matter, the authors are naturally faced with a technical problem, which Palma never had, of making their dialogue reflect the characters' social and educational levels. Each author has a different way of dealing with the matter.

A comparison of López Albújar's and García Calderón's recording of Indian speech is especially interesting. To be absolutely authentic, of course, an author would have the Peruvian Indian speak mostly in Quechua. The reason for not doing so is obvious; therefore, another solution must be found which will preserve both coherence and credibility. García Calderón resorts to a peculiar sort of pidgin Spanish when his Indian characters speak, so that their limited sentences consist mainly of a subject and a present participle: *"Tu esperando," "Yo riclimando taita," "su alma yéndose no más,"* etc. This device is unsatisfactory since, instead of contributing to the authenticity of the characters, it has quite the opposite effect of reinforcing the stereotype. López Albújar, on the other hand, makes little or no effort to create a special language for his Indian characters. While certainly not using flawless Spanish, they are able to express themselves fluently and with some subtlety. The effect is satisfactory, for although the dialogue is not authentic, it serves to make the characters stand out as individuals who can be taken seriously within the context of the stories. Fortunately, García Calderón was much more successful in recording the characteristic speech habits of the Negro and mulatto peons of the coast. His accurate representation of their pronunciation and idiomatic usage adds authenticity to the stories even though these characters play only minor roles.

All three authors use a variety of local and American terms such as *chicha de bonita, coca, guagua, tambo, chacchando, quena, taita, huacos,* etc. It is important to point out, however, that these terms are either used within a context which leaves their meaning clear to any reader, or else they are clarified by a brief explanation, often in parentheses, after the word in question. Furthermore, such usage does not place the narratives strictly within the category of local color or *criollismo*. While careful use of native words and local expressions lends special national flavor, the intent and effect of the stories differ from later, highly regionalistic narratives, where the detailed presentation of local types, customs, and speech habits is the very heart of the works.

As for economy—the extent to which the author implies rather than specifies in order to preserve necessary brevity in the narrative—Valdelomar, López Albújar, and García Calderón use essentially the same measures as Palma: limited descriptions of character and setting, a limited number of characters, and initiation of action close to the point of climax. In other words, all three authors try to be explicit only in details which contribute to the forward motion of the action. Valdelomar and López Albújar are especially fond of dividing their narratives into short, numbered scenes, as Palma does, in order to take advantage of the convenient skips of time between scenes. Both Valdelomar and López Albújar are talented at quickly and efficiently establishing the conflict within the first section. Without question, however, García Calderón, whose stories are considerably more compact than any studied so far, is the master of economy. Each of his narratives is a perfect example of quick capturing of reader interest, concise exposition, skillful foreshadowing, and impact-filled climax. The ability to accomplish these ends in a limited space reflects not only his knowledge of short story technique but also his unusual command of language.

Valdelomar, López Albújar, and García Calderón reach the zenith of their careers as far as their short story production is concerned during the so-called era of *postmodernismo* in Peru, a period particularly alive with aesthetic currents which are conflicting in some circumstances and complementary in others. Literary groups and societies with avowedly different interests and goals may reflect common influences or even overlap in their activities. The case of the three authors in question is no exception to this crazy-quilt pattern. García Calderón is chronologically and aesthetically a member of the *generación novecentista* headed by José de la Riva Agüero, a group which was at once politically conservative, interested in scholarly research, in the diffusion of traditional culture, and in the cultivation of an elegant lucid writing style. Valdelomar, on the other hand, belongs to a slightly later group known as *Colónida*, which, interestingly enough, was in part a rebellion against the conservatism of the *novecentistas*. At the same time, however, its members were also concerned with many of the same literary and stylistic refinements as the group they were opposed to. López Albújar, the oldest of the three, belongs chronologically to the *modernista* generation of Chocano and Clemente Palma and, early in his career, formed part of the *Pablo de Olavide* literary society which was most active at the turn of the century. His longevity and sensitivity to change, however, have made him a figure of continuing significance throughout the twentieth century, beginning with his earliest *fin de siècle* works, reaching a high point with his national stories of the twenties, and terminating with his urban narratives in the fifties.

Despite the divergency of Valdelomar's, López Albújar's, and García Calderón's literary positions and affiliations, their relationship, as it pertains to the history of Peruvian fiction, is remarkably close. Each possesses the vivid imagination and other intangible qualities which make a great writer. To these natural talents, they add a thorough knowledge of the modern short story technique. A fundamental common denominator is also found in the general division of their narrative production according to stories of cosmopolitan setting and those with a Peruvian background. Their works in the latter category contain their greatest literary and historical contributions. In their common and contemporaneous incorporation of rural settings and characters within the framework of the modern short story, they set a pattern for Peruvian writers which held sway until the fifties.

# III

## LOCAL COLOR AND
## SOCIAL PROTEST

THE SHORT STORY writers prominent during the late twenties, thirties, and forties seek their inspiration in the national scene. Like Valdelomar, López Albújar, and García Calderón before them, they are concerned with the settings and characters of rural Peru; but their focus is sharper and more sensitive to surface detail as they strive to record with photographic accuracy local topography, customs, speech habits, and racial types. Because of this preoccupation, many of the stories are noticeably narrow and concentrated in scope. For example, the reader may be introduced in detail to the provincial ways of an isolated farming community in the Marañón area or to life in the remote jungle region around Saposoa. He may learn of the superstitions and economic endeavors of a group of Lake Titicaca Indians or of the dialect and daily activities of mulatto families who work on coastal plantations. Considered as a whole the abundant information supplied by these stories provides a complete, almost documentary picture of the wide diversity of Peruvian landscapes and peoples.

Social protest is also an important element in many of the narratives written during these years. Their main concern is the wretched socioeconomic condition of the Peruvian Indian, and the procedure used almost exclusively by the protesting authors is to contrast the downtrodden Indians with their cruel oppressors—unscrupulous clergymen, wealthy landlords, and corrupt government officials—who work to preserve the status quo with total disregard for justice or the law. Some of the stories emphasize the idea of class struggle and call for an end to the sociopolitical system which perpetuates the unfavorable conditions. Social protest usually dominates these stories, but among them are some works where the author gives equal attention to the detailing of native customs and local color.

The persistent sense of national concern that characterizes most of the stories written during this period obviously owes much to Valdelomar, López Albújar, and García Calderón, whose works so magnificiently incorporate rural Peruvian settings and characters. But this concern deepened and developed under the influence of other factors which should be briefly noted. World War I served to encourage a widespread surge of nationalistic fervor that had a strong, if belated, impact in Peru as well as in the rest of Latin America in the late twenties.[1] Some of the writers more specifically preoccupied with their country's economic problems and social injustices were influenced by another international phenomenon—the growth of Marxism. Communism was not embraced completely or wholeheartedly, even by the more militant; however, certain Marxist doctrines and solutions held —and continue to hold—a special, if limited attraction. The greatest single factor in the deepening awareness of national problems and of native Peruvian culture was the impulse given by Manuel González Prada (1848–1919) who prodded the consciences of his fellow countrymen with his speeches and essays. At the turn of the century when Peru had reached an almost unbelievable state of political and economic chaos as a result of the corruption of its leaders, the indifference of its intellectuals, and the ignorance of its common people, this great writer and reformer began his mission of awakening

Peruvians to their need for self-knowledge and self-discipline. Eventually his admonitions had an impact on the country as a whole; ultimately he was also able to show many aspiring writers, some of whom came into literary prominence during the late twenties and thirties, that they had a social as well as an artistic responsibility to their reading public.[2] González Prada provided little in the way of a specific program or political philosophy for the improvement of his country, but what he did was more significant and far-reaching. He encouraged a serious concern for national heritage and national problems that has not ceased to influence Peruvian intellectuals to this day.

### *The* Amauta *Writers*

Closely related to the influences just outlined is the emergence in the late twenties of a group of literary men and women whom we will call the *Amauta* writers. These writers initially come into prominence through articles or stories which appear in a famous Peruvian periodical by that name, and, to a greater or lesser extent, each reflects the spirit and ideals of José Carlos Mariátegui (1895–1930), its founder.

Mariátegui, one of González Prada's most illustrious disciples, is considered by some commentators to have been the greatest single political and literary influence in Peru during the twenties.[3] He was born in Lima into a family whose economic situation was precarious and he knew what it was to be short of food and ill-clothed. At twelve he had to go to work in a printing shop where he suffered a permanent injury to his right leg. Largely self-educated, he spent all his spare time reading. At sixteen, he was correcting manuscripts sent him by established authors. By the time he was eighteen, he had become a close friend of such writers as Gibson, Vallejo, Valdelomar, and Falcón and had begun to contribute articles of his own to local newspapers and magazines. By 1917, César Falcón, a journalist who sought to interest Peruvian intellectuals in his advanced labor and economic ideas, had begun to influence Mariátegui. In 1918, they were both given a free trip to Europe by the Leguía government. This action was not without ulterior motive, for Leguía was disturbed by the possibility of these young writers spreading radical notions and saw the trip abroad as a gentle but effective means of getting them out of the way for awhile.

Mariátegui traveled about Europe for four years, carefully observing the progress of Marxism there. In 1923, he returned, a firm believer in Marxist doctrine, to a Peru where labor was in ferment, the universities were struggling for reform, and Haya de la Torre was emerging as the great advocate of APRA, the Alianza Popular Revolucionaria Americana. *Aprista* cells were appearing in several Latin American countries, including Peru, where Mariátegui became one of the important leaders.[4] Within this environment of general political, social, and economic unrest, he began to make his influence felt through articles which advocated radical changes in the socioeconomic structure of his country. His home became a regular meeting place for artists, writers, labor leaders, and students.

In September of 1926, Mariátegui founded *Amauta*, which flourished with minor interruptions until 1930.[5] This unique publication included a wide variety of subjects ranging from literary criticism to economic studies. Besides devoting space to poetry, short stories, and novelettes, the journal also published articles on science, geography, politics, art, and history. The editors welcomed contributions from writers at home and abroad, from eager beginners as well as established authors. Above all, *Amauta* reflected the spirit and ideals of its founder who stated that one of the major objectives of that publication was to provide a deeper understanding of Peru.[6] This goal was of particular importance to Peruvian contributors who sought earnestly for a national identity by studying their country's heritage and asking what could be done to improve her future. A vital concern for Mariátegui, encompassed within the larger objective, was the Indian problem. He vigorously attacked the feudalistic system which had made the Indians virtual slaves and called for a restoration of their ancient Inca dignity.

The ideas and challenges propounded by Mariátegui strongly influenced the *Amauta* writers' short story production during the late twenties. Thus, the feudalistic land tenure system, the poor working conditions and health standards of coastal haciendas, and the exaltation of Inca customs—points which Mariátegui stressed in his essays and speeches—were themes which appeared in their Indianist narratives. The larger concern of knowing Peru better caused the authors to focus with intensity on specific rural regions and groups and their way of life. Local color and social protest became the very heart of these stories, taking precedence over plot, characterization, and other artistic considerations. Thus many of the narratives are more notable for their didactic and tendentious qualities than for their literary merits.

María Wiesse (1894–1964), biographer of *Amauta's* colorful and influential founder, considered the short story her favorite literary form. She was born in Lima, but at the age of four traveled with her family to Europe where she received her education in exclusive schools in Switzerland and England. As a young girl she returned to Lima and completed her formal education in Peru. In 1922 she married José Sabogal, a well-known artist who is generally credited with having introduced the element of Indianism into modern Peruvian painting. Upon Mariátegui's return from Europe in 1923, the couple became frequent visitors at his home and were among those who encouraged him to found *Amauta*.[7] María Wiesse's career as an author dates from the appearance of that periodical, and her first short stories were published within its pages in 1928 and 1929.

Two of these narratives, "El forastero" and "El veneno," are particularly noteworthy because they propound in a fictional manner two of Mariátegui's main theses concerning land reform and the Indian problem. Convinced that the traditional form of landholding was hindering Peru's development, he had observed:

The land tenure system in the rural areas of Peru is one of the most formidable obstacles in the way of developing a national capitalism. This obstacle stems primarily from the mistaken economic theories of the large landholder who is interested only in the immediate yield of his land and not in improving its long-range productivity. The system of the absentee landlord and the lack of credit available for the small tenant farmer make matters even worse.\* [8]

María Wiesse incorporates this criticism in "El forastero," which tells of the return of Felipe Morales, son of a prosperous hacienda owner, to his homeland after spending a number of years in Paris where he has acquired an excellent education and become thoroughly familiar with the European way of life. His father is dead, and the hacienda is controlled by his greedy brothers who are interested only in the immediate yield of the land and not its long-range productivity. In their desire for quick profit, they have planted unwisely and ruthlessly squeezed out the tenant farmers around them. Felipe attempts to stop the abuses, but his feeble efforts meet with failure. The "message" of the narrative is obvious: Peru is suffering economically, socially, and morally because unscrupulous landowners are too interested in personal profit to develop their holdings wisely or to give proper opportunity to the small tenant farmers who also have a stake in their country's future. The situation is made worse by those absentee landlords whom Wiesse accuses of having spent the best years of their youth in foreign countries. The well-educated people either wake up too late or not at all to their responsibility to their less fortunate fellow countrymen.

---

\* For original Spanish passages, see pages 170 ff.

Since the prime concern is the exposition of Mariátegui's ideas, little attention is given to such matters as plot or characterization. Indeed, the literary aspect is so secondary as to serve only as a sort of pleasant sugar-coating for the didactic pill. The characters are wooden stereotypes. Felipe represents the basically good, but misguided, group that must be re-oriented, and the ruthless brothers stand for the forces of evil which must be eliminated. As a token gesture to fictional interests, the author includes a love triangle involving Felipe, one of his brothers, and the daughter of a neighbor family. In a climax hardly worthy of the name, Felipe loses out both in his contest for the girl and his attempts to turn the tide of events at the hacienda.

In "El veneno," María Wiesse uses the following pro-nouncement by Mariátegui as her basic narrative theme: "On Peruvian coastal haciendas no attention is paid to the health of the workers. Because of this neglect, malaria is so prevalent that it plays havoc with the rural coastal population which is made up primarily of mestizos and Indians." [9] She makes her point in an obvious manner by describing in detail the ravages of sickness among the peons of a coastal plantation. Most of the victims are Indians from the sierra, who have been lured to the coast by the promises of dishonest white men. Instead of high wages and pleasant jobs, they find inhuman work schedules, unsanitary living conditions, and disease. The conflict of the narrative again derives from the opposing forces of good and evil. On the side of right is Demetrio Paredes, a physician who fights a losing battle against the spread of malaria among the peons. On the other side are the selfish hacienda owners, who either reside in plush mansions or as absentee landlords in the capital, unmoved by the knowledge that their workers exist in abject poverty and filth. Paredes pleads with the owners to change these conditions, but they scoff at him, thus passing up an opportunity to make a concrete contribution to the welfare of their less fortunate

fellow countrymen. Again, literary considerations are only
incidental to the documentary and social reform content of the
story. Righteous indignation is aroused by contrasting the
frustrated, but just, cause of Paredes with the smug cynicism
of those who would block his efforts. In short, the line
between good and evil is clearly drawn, and the wicked—
those who stand in the way of reform—are left without an
excuse or a redeeming feature.

"El forastero" and "El veneno" are included in María
Wiesse's first book of short stories, *Nueve relatos*, published in
1933.[10] The other works in this collection are also primarily
concerned with exposing social injustices and exalting the
indigenous aspects of Peru. Though in subsequent years María
Wiesse occasionally published stories in local newspapers and
magazines, her next collections do not appear until the fifties.
*Pequeñas historias* (1951), *Linterna mágica* (1954), and *El
pez de oro y otras historias* (1958) do not contain the
emphasis on social reform which had generally characterized
the narratives she wrote during her association with *Amauta*.[11]
Some of these later stories are notable for their humor and
psychological insight. She does not, however, completely lose
her penchant for didacticism even in those narratives where
purely artistic considerations are predominant.

Less productive and significant as short story writers than
María Wiesse, but more bitter in their attacks against the
exploiters of the Indian, are César Falcón and Arturo Peralta,
who is better known by his pseudonym, Gamaniel Churata.
During the flourishing years of *Amauta* they worked closely
with Mariátegui, writing novels, short stories, essays, and
poetry which emphasized the idea of class struggle. Whereas
María Wiesse saw within the privileged class a remnant
worthy of salvation if they would but repent, Falcón and
Churata were much less gracious to the oppressors of the
masses. Their stories of the sierra are notable for their virulent
denunciation of the evils of *gamonalismo*, the feudalistic land

tenure system which Mariátegui considered to be the principal factor in the Indians' degradation and in undermining the economy of the country.

Churata's "El gamonal," which appeared in *Amauta* in 1927, is one of the most vehement protests ever registered against Peruvian feudalistic practices.[12] The plot is so thin and the exposition so chaotic as to make a concise summary of the action impossible. Led more by a violent personal reaction to the injustices he perceives than by any narrative plan, the author recounts in abundant but haphazard detail the crimes of murder, rape, exploitation, and bestiality perpetrated against the sierra Indians by their white overlords. Unfortunately, the very absence of restraint and selectivity, and the lack of consideration for the demands of fictional art, militate against credibility and against the sense of immediacy which the author wishes to convey.

One of César Falcón's most representative stories is "Los buenos hijos de Dios."[13] No less biting in its criticism than Churata's narrative, but more skillfully handled, it convincingly depicts the calculated degradation of the Andean Indian by those who wish to keep him in bondage. The plot is so well-fitted to the author's satirical and didactic designs that it is worth recounting in some detail. Because of their superstitious natures and their basic misunderstanding of Church teachings as presented by the local priest, the Indians of a small Andean community come to venerate as a saint a young Indian girl whom they formerly treated with cruelty. Out of fear and respect, the Indians cease their drunken orgies and refuse *aguardiente* which the governor and the local hacienda owners urge them to drink. Despite the ironical reasons for this change of attitude and habit, some positive results are forthcoming. A new spirit of respect for self and for others grips them. They begin to recover their ancient Inca dignity and to stand together for common causes. The cruelty and trickery of the white man are no longer tolerated with abject resignation. When the white landowners, the clergy, and the governmental officials begin to feel the effects of the change, they beg the local priest to do something to restore the Indians to their old ways. He suggests that when the girl passes from the scene all will return to normal. Shortly thereafter, the girl dies under rather suspicious circumstances, and the grieving Indians are persuaded that their saint, now watching over them from heaven, would want them to honor her with a fiesta at which the old intoxicating beverages should be served. The priest's prophecy is soon fulfilled. The Indians once again return to their drunken, disorderly ways and, with the resultant loss of self-respect, fall easy prey to the white man's feudalistic designs. This story is an excellent example of how social protest can be presented with maximum effectiveness. Because of careless exposition and superficial characterization, the work still leaves something to be desired from an artistic point of view; yet it is thoroughly credible because the author has exercised discretion in his choice of details and has avoided moralizing.

Though not primarily known as a short story writer, Emilio Romero is the one who uses the form most effectively in response to Mariátegui's challenge to know Peru better. He was born in Puno in 1899 and completed both his primary and secondary schooling there. Most of his advanced work was done at the University of San Marcos in Lima, where he received his law degree in 1925. During this period he became a friend of Mariátegui and an associate of the *Amauta* group. His subsequent contributions to that periodical were not of a literary nature, but he established a reputation as an excellent writer through his articles on geography, history, economics, and the Indian problem. Romero later went to Arequipa for advanced study in political science and economics, receiving his doctorate from the university there in 1932. That same year he was appointed professor of economics and history at the University of San Marcos where he continues to hold classes.

In the field of literature, Romero's major contributions are his short narratives, seventeen of which were collected for publication under the title *Balseros del Titicaca* (1934).[14] The setting for all of the stories is Lake Titicaca, the region of the author's birth. Although social protest is implicit in some of the narratives, Romero is obviously most concerned with supplying cultural and environmental information. Calling on his personal experience and his scientific knowledge of the region and its people, he presents graphic, accurate portrayals of landscape, customs, beliefs, and superstitions. While the plots are uniformly thin and the characters are simply representative types, the stories come alive through the author's judicious use of regionalistic detail.

"Balseros del Titicaca," title story of the collection, describes the way in which the Indians, who live on the numerous floating islands of the lake, make their living. Largely dependent on the lake and its products, the Indians' most important possessions are primitive, one-man boats used for transportation and fishing. The fishermen usually go out at night to locate a school of fish and then light small bonfires in the boats so that the temporarily blinded fish can be dipped out in nets. Fishing is a tedious, back-breaking operation, often made hazardous by bad weather. The stoic, *coca-*chewing Indian sells his catch for a few cents at Puno, then must set out immediately to repeat the process in order to obtain a meager living.

Interspersed throughout this portrayal of the lake fishermen are descriptions of the flora and fauna. Romero recognizes that environmental features, properly selected and arranged in a work of fiction, can provide a unique insight into a region. At the same time, he understands that landscape description must be properly related to action and characterization if a narrative is going to be more than a simple sketch. In other words, the background description should influence the action and provide a greater understanding of the characters' activities within their physical environment. In this story, conflict, rising tension, and climax all derive directly from the exciting episode of a storm during which the author abruptly narrows his focus to one man's desperate struggle against the elements. Within the framework of general information, this very personal episode provides a special vision of the relationship that Lake Titicaca Indians have with their surroundings.

In addition to his portrayal of the Indians' working customs, Romero uses such stories as "Ttacko," "Viejo granizo," and "Buscando la yunta" to describe some of their beliefs and superstitious practices. The setting for the first story is again the lake, and the main character is an Indian who makes his living by ferrying people in his boat. Two white men, one a foreigner full of questions, are used by the author as a device to show the fascinating, and often amusing, superstitions held by the Indian ferrymen. Before embarking, the Indian throws a handful of *coca* into the wind and intones a short prayer for a favorable crossing. However, he frankly informs his passengers that the prayer has little chance of being answered since just minutes before a *bandurria* crossed his path. When an Indian encounters this lake bird just before crossing, it means that he will be caught in a *ttacko,* that is, the wind will die down completely, leaving him becalmed and often at the mercy of the broiling sun. Another superstition is revealed when the foreign passenger throws the remains of his lunch overboard. The frightened Indian explains that this action will surely cause a disaster. Finally, the ferryman observes the ultimate in bad omens when another water bird, a *tordo,* perches on the sail of the boat. Romero's main purpose, of course, is to show some of the Titicaca Indians' curious beliefs; but not forgetting the exigencies of fictional art, he uses these same beliefs to aid in the stage by stage development of the story. Each omen is in turn a foreshadowing of possible crises to come, thus promoting the forward motion of the action and helping to sustain reader interest.

In "Viejo granizo" Romero writes about the Indians who farm the plateau regions bordering the lake. It is harvest time and the reader is given typical pictures of men and women at work in the fields. Flirtations are carried on among the younger Indians, the boy demonstrating his interest with the time-honored method of throwing pebbles at the girl of his choice. Again the story focuses on the struggle between man and nature. The main action centers around the Indians' efforts to "frighten away" a hailstorm which could ruin the year's harvest and bring starvation. Bonfires are lighted, and the Indians frantically dance about them shouting their supplications until at last the storm clouds drift away.

Finally, in "Buscando la yunta," Romero shows the Indians' blind faith in the powers of a soothsayer or witch doctor. In almost every area of the sierra there are old men or women who are believed to have special powers. Natives from miles around come to consult them about everything from sickness to unrequited love. This story concerns a young couple who have lost their oxen. They set off for the nearest witch doctor and hopefully enlist his aid. Resolutely following his every order, they soon find the animals and return home even more steadfast in their belief than before their experience.

These examples are representative of Romero's short stories. Obviously, his main concern is to portray the characteristics of a limited area and its inhabitants. His preoccupation with surface reality causes him to describe people and places very precisely, sometimes in the terminology of a social scientist. At the same time, however, Romero's stories are artistically satisfactory as well as informative because of his concern for literary discipline.

In the short stories produced by the *Amauta* writers we see an intensification of interest in Peru. The search for national identity and the concern for contemporary social truth cause the authors to emphasize the unique characteristics of their country as well as to examine its problems critically. Concurrent with the sharp focus on regionalistic elements and social protest is a general de-emphasis of purely literary concerns. Most obviously neglected are plot and characterization. The characters are uniformly lacking in psychological depth; the authors seem to know much about their characters without really knowing them. The plot is often submerged under a welter of propaganda or prosaic detail. Despite these artistic limitations, however, the stories are informative and significant as literary reflections of a society and its problems.

## Writers of the Thirties

The writers of the thirties add considerably to the record of Peruvian cultural and environmental diversity with their short story production. Their main interest continues to be the depiction of unique rural settings and provincial character types. It should be noted, however, that of this group there are those who strive, successfully, to comply also with the demands of fictional art. One is José Diez-Canseco (1904–49), an able craftsman of the short story form as well as a capable portrayer of regional peculiarities. He was born in Lima and received part of his education at the Colegio de los Padres Jesuitas. Before completing his studies, he left school and tried a variety of jobs, including newspaper work. In 1928 he became a columnist for *El Tiempo*. Between 1931 and 1934 he spent a period of exile in Europe where he continued his journalistic activities in collaboration with *Candide, Le Journal de Paris, A B C* of Madrid, and other leading periodicals.

Like many other Latin American writers, Diez-Canseco combined his occupation as a journalist with a serious interest in belles-lettres. In 1929 and 1930 two of his novelettes, *El gaviota* and *El km. 83*, were published. These works, which portray in a sympathetic manner the *zambo* or mulatto culture of coastal Peru, enjoyed immediate critical acclaim and were shortly thereafter published in a single volume with the subtitle *Estampas mulatas*.[15] In addition to his novelettes,

Diez-Canseco left a large body of writings unpublished or dispersed in the newspapers and magazines to which he contributed. His widow has collected many of these works for publication,[16] but much gathering and editing of other stories remains to be done.

In 1938 *Estampas mulatas* was published again, this time with a new section containing four of his best stories.[17] An enlarged edition of this work including three stories which had not previously appeared in collected form was published in 1951.[18] All of these narratives have in common their rural settings and their *cholo* and *zambo* characters.[19] Such remote, provincial locales of the coast and sierra as Huarmey, Huacho, Pacarán, and Yauyos form the background for lively dramas acted out by petty municipal officials, mulatto peons, small hacienda owners, humble store proprietors, and outlaws. The peaceful, fun-loving side of these people is seen in their daily activities and traditional celebrations; a less peaceful side is also shown in their direct, often violent resolution of personal differences. Their primitive and vigorous approach to all aspects of life obviously attracted the author who, while making no attempt to gloss over the social, moral, and educational shortcomings of his provincial characters, exalted their vitality and capacity for enjoyment.

*Criollismo,* the *criollo* "spirit" or "way of life," is an aspect of the Peruvian mestizo culture which Diez-Canseco captures with special sensitivity. The term *criollo* has a variety of meanings within the general Latin American cultural context. In Peru, as Ozzie Simmons has correctly stated, it has come to refer to a special cultural outlook held by the mestizo:

As an adjective, criollo is associated only with the cholo, the Negro, or the zambo, but never with the indígena. A cholo may be classified as more or less criollo, depending on the degree of his orientation to the criollo outlook, but an indígena (i.e., as defined by the mestizo) is considered far removed from *criollismo.* . . . The term criollo may be used in a nationalistic, an ethnic, a status,

or a regional sense, but all of these are related manifestations, on
different levels, of the criollo outlook. The essence of this outlook
is its explicit affirmation of the uniqueness and originality of the
mestizo culture. . . . [It is] a sort of elusive *weltanschauung* that
cannot in itself be concretely defined, but which stamps mestizo
culture and mestizo personality with a particular identity and
integrity of their own. Criollismo is the mestizo's answer to the
painful question of who and what he is, his assertion that his "way
of life" is a positive creation of his own rather than a casual
European-indigenous mixture.[20]

Diez-Canseco describes in a faithful and detailed manner
such external aspects of *criollismo* as the food, drink, dancing,
music, and forms of celebration. In "Chicha, mar y bonito," for
example, the typical dishes are enumerated: *cebiche de
bonito encebollado y picante* (fish prepared in a highly
seasoned way), *choclos* (corn), *camotes* (sweet potatoes), and
*yucas* (manioc). "El velorio" describes a wake which quickly
—and typically—degenerates into an uninhibited *jarana*
(fiesta) where the mourners drink Peruvian *claro* (brandy),
*chicha* (corn beer), and dance the traditional *marinera* and
*vals criollo* to the accompaniment of the indispensable box
drum and guitar. The *marinera*, which symbolizes the court-
ing of the female by the male, is considered to be especially
*criollo*,[21] and it encourages the improvization of roguish lyrics
spiced with irony and *double-entendre*.

Besides the external symbols of *criollismo*, Diez-Canseco
also describes its personal and psychological manifestations.
One of its more interesting aspects is a picaresque, sometimes
malicious quality of humor. A hint of it is seen in the lyrics of
certain *criollo* songs; it carries over at a more complex level to
conversations and personal relationships where the cunning,
cutting verbal jab and the capacity for astute trickery are both
practiced and admired. In "Don Salustiano Merino, notario,"
Diez-Canseco records the subtle, taunting wit of the patrons
of a village tavern who, with a great show of innocence,
needle their crony, an elderly notary, because of his unsuc-

cessful courtship of a young girl. Salustiano is, in fact, fast losing out to a younger, more attractive rival, and for that reason, the barbs of his drinking companions are the more painful. The following is an example of one of the verbal exchanges in which the rival is referred to slyly.

With a great show of innocence, the smiling Don Evaristo Claro commented: "An engineer has arrived at the Poderosa mine. He is still a young fellow—quite young. He couldn't be more than thirty. And it seems that in the two months that he has been in the area he has really been getting around—living it up you might say."

"Oh?"

"And they tell me—of course, I don't know for sure myself—that every Friday night he comes down to Pacarán instead of staying at the mining camp. I'm only repeating what I've heard, of course."

Merino smiled in turn: "It must be because it's too cold for him there. You know how it is up in the *puna*. And these young softies from Lima begin to whimper and complain the minute they're away from their mamas. Right?"

"Some of them, yes; others no. And in the case of this young fellow we don't really know what kind of stuff he's made of."

The notary bristled at the allusion. "What are you driving at Don Evaristo?"

"Me? Why nothing at all." (p. 105)

Given the incongruity of the situation and the veiled yet obvious intention of the characters, the scene is not without its humorous side. At the same time, the author has also caught the typically malicious flavor of the commentary. In turn, Salustiano reacts in a manner that is also characteristic of the *criollo* spirit by having his opponent killed in such a way that no incriminating evidence is left, yet lets everyone know that he has avenged his honor. The triumph is thus scored in a shrewd, dramatic fashion and the taunting companions are properly silenced.

The dramatic and out-of-the-ordinary overcoming of an opponent so admired in the *criollo* culture is also interestingly depicted in Diez-Canseco's prize-winning story "Jijuna." [22] In this case the triumph is "bloodless," but nonetheless stunning and appealing to the *criollo* temperament, as a young outlaw responds to the threats of an older, well-established hacienda owner by waging a daring and successful war of nerves against him. In both stories, the author stresses as a significant cultural trait of his characters their admiration for the ability to displace an opponent who is temporarily in the ascendancy. However, this admiration should not be confused with simple "rooting for the underdog." The dramatic quality and shrewdness of the triumph, not the characters involved, are the major considerations, and fair play and honesty are of no importance.

Of all the Peruvians that Diez-Canseco portrayed in his stories, his favorites were the *zambos*. He not only knew these people well, but, as we see expressed in this letter to Benjamín Carrión, had a special sympathy for them: "I think and feel like a *zambo*. Once I had to pawn my ring at a wild party in Callao in order to tempt with *pisco* a dark-skinned young beauty who was dancing to the passionate strains of a *tondero*. And there I remain—even when I am in Paris—among those enticing mulattos, in that illustrious citadel of *criollos*, embracing my guitar while I make love to the darlings." [23]

In delineating his mulatto characters, Diez-Canseco emphasizes their vigor, their capacity for enjoyment within the most simple surroundings, and the volatile nature of their emotions. The young men are able to do hard manual labor under the intense coastal sun after an all night party of dancing and drinking. The young women are physically attractive and equally vigorous in their approach to life. The love between man and woman has a markedly physical, sensuous flavor. Their liaisons are usually not formalized by either church or civil ceremony; however, the author emphasizes the essentially innocent and happy quality of their relationships. Leopoldo and Isolina, the main characters of "El velorio," are

Diez-Canseco's most fully developed models of the healthy, passionate, but innocent, *zambo* culture. In a sense, they are idealized, almost romantic types: Isolina, the beautiful, faithful wife who lives only to enjoy and give pleasure to her husband; Leopoldo, the handsome, protective husband who would kill the man who dared to insult his wife. However, they are not idealized to the point that we do not see their limited vision of life and the basic poverty of their surroundings, nor are they simply faceless reflections of their society. Though having no real profundity of personality, they do possess a vigor and authenticity which enable us to think of them as individuals, as well as representatives of a culture.

Diez-Canseco chooses the theme of vengeance to show the mulattos' direct, uninhibited method of solving personal differences. In "El velorio" and "Chicha, mar y bonito" where the conflict stems from an affair of honor involving a woman, the *zambos'* concept of justice is remarkably like that of the Indian as portrayed by López Albújar. They feel that the scales of justice can only be balanced by a fitting, personal revenge. In both of Diez-Canseco's stories, the aggrieved party achieves his revenge through a violent, man-to-man confrontation with the offender.

Although Diez-Canseco is obviously concerned with local color and with providing an original and authentic insight into a fundamental aspect of Peruvian culture, his attitude toward literature is different from that of the preceding *Amauta* writers. He accepts the author's responsibility to record his environment faithfully, but shys away from political preoccupations. In a prologue to *Estampas mulatas,* he states his position:

I thought then, as I do now, that a literary man, in the noblest sense of that term, ought to be a complete agnostic as far as politics are concerned. To be sure, a writer can and should describe the atmosphere and social environment in which he lives; that is, he should be a social writer. I don't believe, however, that

an author should allow his artistic production to be shaped by
political considerations. . . . Life, after all, is not made up of
political parties. Love, hate, jealousy, adventure, son and father
are identical in the Soviet Union, under Fascism, or under Nazism.
For this reason, it seems absurd to me to attempt to depict
political preoccupations artistically. It is much better to deal with
the subject directly in a book on politics, in a speech, or in a
manifesto. To deal with political matters in a poem or a novel is
unthinkable. (p. 11)

In his short stories, Diez-Canseco is always consistent with
this statement of belief. Propaganda, the plea for social
reform, and protest are completely absent. Implicit in his
whole statement is his belief in the importance of artistic
considerations within literature. In none of his obviously
regionalistic stories does he ever allow the interests of local
color to overshadow plot and characterization, nor does he
overlook the importance of such technical matters as structure
and exposition.

Like Diez-Canseco, Fernando Romero is also able to
combine accurate portrayals of the inhabitants and environmental peculiarities of rural Peru with proper attention to the
short story craft. He was born in Lima in 1905 and received all
of his formal education there, including a doctorate from the
University of San Marcos. After his university studies, he
joined the Peruvian navy and took part in a special explora-
tory study of the nation's jungle waterways during the early
thirties. There can be little doubt that these travel experiences
and the opportunity to observe fellow Peruvians from all areas
and walks of life influenced greatly the content and dimension
of his short stories. Romero resigned his naval commision in
the early forties to enter the field of education as a career.
Besides working as a professor, he held high administrative
positions in the Ministry of Education and has been rector of
the University of Huamanga in Ayacucho.

Romero's list of publications is lengthy and varied. It
includes technical manuals on the complicated functions of a

warship, cultural studies about the Negro and mulatto, and numerous articles on education. His chief claim to fame as a writer, however, rests on his vernacular short stories which depict the customs, speech habits, and often violent activities of the Indian, mestizo, and mulatto inhabitants of the Peruvian coast and jungle. Most of these narratives are found in *Doce novelas de la selva* (1934) and *Mar y playa* (1940).[24] The latter collection, which contains his best works, has the coast as a common setting and introduces a fascinating gallery of beachcombers, sailors, fishermen, and petty government officials.

Two of the selections from *Mar y Playa*, "Maritierra" and "Santos Tarqui," make an interesting and significant complement to Diez-Canseco's stories because of their mulatto characters and their presentation of the *criollo* spirit. In the first story we meet Willy Villamonte, a *zambo* fisherman, who, in the words of the author is a real he-man, a tough customer at sea or on dry land. He is, in fact, the embodiment of all the major *criollo* attributes: uninhibited at play, always ready with the ironic, malicious jest, skilled at tricking an opponent, and ready to take direct, violent action if the need arises. Character conflict and hence the whole plot complication stem directly from the fatal clash between Willy's *criollo* attitude and activities and the attitude and responsibility of Pedro Salas, officer of the port. Their personal duel is mildly amusing in the early stages, but eventually it assumes savage proportions, ending in tragedy for both of them.

In "Santos Tarqui" the author pursues the same theme, but this time without a hint of humor, since the conflict between the main characters, Narváez, a coastal mulatto, and Tarqui, a sierra Indian, is more far-reaching and serious in its social implications. Their clash goes beyond a limited collision of personal interests; it represents the confrontation of two cultures, each incomprehensible to the other. The opponents have in common their occupations as seamen and their primitive way of solving human conflict in a direct, personal, and, if necessary, violent way. Beyond this there are no points of similarity. The characteristics of *criollismo* are strongly apparent in Narváez, a shrewd, ingenious rogue with a silver tongue and a penchant for getting away with something whenever possible. Tarqui, on the other hand, is withdrawn, serious in his approach to all aspects of life from work to human relationships. The irony of the situation is that the characters, precisely because of their cultural backgrounds and limited horizons, cannot see their conflict for what it is. Tarqui is unable to appreciate the innocence of Narváez' gregariousness or the unpremeditated quality of his words and deeds. Narváez is oblivious to the seriousness with which Tarqui interprets those words and deeds. The tragic end is made inevitable when the two are forced to work together in the close confines of the engine room of a ship. Narváez' volatile, outgoing nature causes him to bring his feelings out into the open, enabling him to maintain a degree of equilibrium. Tarqui nurses his resentment to the point where he can no longer restrain himself. He attacks his antagonist, knocking him into an open boiler. Though the conflict is based on obvious and well-known cultural differences and the reactions of one character to the other are readily predictable, the story is, nonetheless, rich in psychological insight. Especially well developed is the character of Tarqui. He is a man who does much of his living inside himself, and the author builds logically and consistently on this trait by letting the reader observe the inner processes—his interpretations, his worries, his building resentment—which lead to the climax. By contrast, we see far less of Narváez' mind, but again, the author is being consistent with the essentially outgoing personality of his character.

Another man who does much of his living "on the inside" is Santos Paucha, the hero of "El nido extraño," Romero's most successful story as far as psychological development of character is concerned. Santos is a humble government worker who barely ekes out an existence for his wife and son by protecting and keeping a count of the guan birds in a remote sector of the coast. The family is very close, but the time comes when the son wishes to leave his parents and start a home of his own. The symbolism of the young birds leaving their nests at the appointed time to gain their independence is subtly and effectively used by the author; but the most remarkable aspect of the narrative, and the heart of the story, is the sensitive portrayal of the inner emotions of a loving father who realizes that his boy has become a man. Santos is a representative type of rural, coastal Peru in terms of his job, customs, and speech; but, because of the intimate glimpse we receive of his mind and character, he takes on an individuality and psychological depth which is remarkable, especially within the confines of a short story.

The jungle provides a totally different setting for *Doce novelas de la selva*, Romero's first collection of stories. They lack the dramatic force of the narratives in *Mar y playa*, particularly in comparison to the three stories just discussed. While recognizing the superiority of Romero's later writings, we are still able to admire the interesting plots and fascinating characters of his jungle stories. These tales have an unusual unifying force—the author's view of the *selva* as a dynamic influence that assumes the role of an omnipresent, fate-deciding character within the stories. Romero elaborates on this view in a brief, prefatory essay to his tales:

The feeling of sadness which runs through the pages of my book is going to be very noticeable. And it will seem odd to the person who has only learned about the South American jungle from books or second-hand information; that is, who has not lived there. But he who has traveled its paths or navigated its rivers will understand perfectly why these are not happy stories. The jungle is a sad place, and everything in it contributes to its being that way. . . . (p. 18)

Within its confines we feel physically and morally small. We are
sad and frightened because everything here lies in wait for us: the
dry leaves that we walk on, the tree that shades us from the sun,
the trunk we lean against, the water we drink, and the fruit which
tempts us. Each one of these simple, vital things which by
themselves could offer us protection, when united in the jungle,
are poised to attack and destroy us. The snake darts out
treacherously, the leaves give off noxious fumes, the tree trunks
harbor destructive insects, the water contains deadly germs, the
fruit poisons us, and the animals attack us. We even contribute to
our own distress. Our excited imaginations cause us to see
supernatural beings which harass and trick us. They are the
demons of the jungle. They are innumerable and cruel.

If even the figments of our own imaginations plague us, how is it
possible to find happiness in the jungle? (pp. 22–23)

The heroes in Romero's stories are determined and resourceful, but their position is, at best, precarious in this
unpredictable and hazardous environment. The jungle can be
a violent, aggressive foe that strikes down a man suddenly and
unexpectedly; it can also be a subtle enemy that slowly erodes
both the physical and spiritual strength of its unsuspecting
human opponent. In "El abrazo," one of the author's most
exciting narratives, man is pitted in a losing battle against the
stealth and ferocity of the animal world. In "La creciente," a
slower-moving but psychologically more complex story, the
hero, well-aware of both the wealth and danger of the jungle,
tries to hold his environmental adversary at bay long enough
to win his fortune. Ironically, however, that region which he
plans so carefully to exploit and then abandon saps him first of
his physical energy through treacherous, debilitating fevers
and finally destroys his very will to return to civilization. "De
regreso" also tells of the jungle's capacity to overpower
psychologically its human adversaries, those who would exploit its resources. The hero, who returns to civilization to
show off his fortune, is allowed to believe temporarily that he
has triumphed in the struggle. However, the jungle has so
thoroughly molded his attitudes and formed his way of life

that he is drawn submissively and fatally back to the environment he had thought to escape. Finally, in "Las tangaranas," the loneliness and physical passion which the jungle inspires wrecks a friendship and leads to the ultimate destruction of those who had seemingly come to terms with their environment. Other stories of this collection do not depict the struggle between man and his natural surroundings in quite so obvious a manner, but the jungle as a pervading, influential force is nonetheless evident.

Romero, like Diez-Canseco, accepted what he considered to be the artist's responsiblility to faithfully record his environment. His interest in bringing various aspects of Peru to the attention of the Peruvians so they might know their country better is evident in the content of his stories and personally affirmed in the introductions to his two major collections. He says in *Mar y playa*:

I want the eight stories which are presented here to be classified as Peruvian. Their purpose is to depict this vast geographic area which is ours—a territory that is divided into distinct regions. I charge them, as in the case of my previous stories, with the responsibility of helping us as Peruvians to understand our own country better. (p. 8)

Again like Diez-Canseco, he saw the writer as having an equal responsibility to maintain artistic standards. For that reason, and also because of his natural abilities as a craftsman of the narrative, his stories are typified not only by local color, but also by vital characters, interesting plots, and careful structures.[25]

Arturo Burga Freitas is less talented and productive as a short story writer than Diez-Canseco and Romero, but is worthy of brief attention because his *selva* tales make an interesting addition to the body of literature pertaining to that area of Peru. He was born in the jungle city of Iquitos in 1909 and received his early schooling there. In 1929 he moved to Lima to enroll in the University of San Marcos. When the university was closed in 1932, he traveled to Santiago and, subsequently, to Buenos Aires. While in the latter city he began his writing career, collaborating actively with the magazines *Crítica, Mundo Argentino, El Hogar,* and the news-paper *La Nación.* Upon returning to Iquitos in 1934, he founded a periodical entitled *Amazonia.* In 1939 he re-entered the University of San Marcos where he received a doctorate in economics. Afterwards, he made a series of statistical studies of the Amazon area for the university. In recent years he has held diplomatic posts in Chile, Brazil, Argentina, and the United States.

Burga Freitas has written one novel and innumerable articles on subjects of social, political, and economic interest. His best known work, however, is a collection of short stories entitled *Ayahuasca, mitos y leyendas del Amazonas* (1939).[26] As the title implies, most of the selections are based on local legends and myths. In some instances the legends and myths are placed within a remote historical context, as in "El árbol de las lágrimas de sangre" and "Inca Dios"; in other instances they are given a contemporary context and are interwoven with the actions of modern visitors and inhabitants of the jungle ("El maligno," "La yara"). A typical feature of all the narratives is the accurate description of flora and fauna and the proper use of jungle terminology. The author also gives a prominent place in these stories to the sights, odors, and sounds of the *selva,* constantly alerting the reader's senses to the endless, surging activity of the animal and vegetable life in the jungle.

Like Romero, Burga Freitas at times envisions the jungle as a hostile region that surrounds man, especially the exploiter, with a myriad of lurking, potentially fatal, physical dangers. This view is well developed in "Los buscadores de oro negro," which depicts the hazardous and often short life of the rubber gatherers. The author is a man whose spirit is attuned to the mysterious forces of the region as well as its hostility. From childhood he observed and heard about the inexplicable happenings that took place there and saw the strange effect that it had on the minds of many who lived within its confines. In "El maligno" and "La yara," he presents this mysterious quality of the jungle and its psychological influence on human intruders. Attacking the characters' minds through strange noises, exotic odors, and weird sights, the jungle provokes fear, uncontrollable desires, and emotional breakdown. Burga Freitas is at his best in these two stories where he is able to blur effectively the line between reality and fantasy. The fearful and fantastic forces of the *selva,* which first lurk on the perimeter of the scene and subsequently intrude to victimize the main characters, can be explained rationally; however, the author is also careful to leave room for other interpretations which provide the bases for fascinating legends.

The coast forms a much more prosaic background for the short stories of María Rosa Macedo. She was born in Pisco in 1912 and spent much of her childhood on a hacienda near that small port town. Like Burga Freitas, she had the advantage of rich personal experience to draw on in formulating her narratives. In 1930 she enrolled in the Escuela de Bellas Artes in Lima to study sculpture, but soon discovered that she was more interested in a writing career. She first entered the journalistic field in a rather limited way by contributing to local periodicals, but as the decade progressed she became a regular and respected writer for newspapers and magazines all over Latin America.

María Rosa Macedo's first major fictional publication was *Ranchos de Caña* (1941), a collection of short stories in which her talents as a careful observer and interpreter of the coast and its inhabitants are displayed.[27] Concentrating on hacienda life, she depicts the customs, superstitions, work habits, entertainment, and speech peculiarities of the humble mulatto, mestizo, and Indian peons. Unlike her contemporaries, Diez-Canseco, Romero, and Burga Freitas, she pays little

attention to plot development or characterization in her
stories. In this respect, she is reminiscent of Emilio Romero of
the *Amauta* group, for her main objective is to record the
provincial ways of a limited social group which she knows
well. Unlike Romero, however, she does not make social
protest even an implicit aspect of her works.

One of her most representative stories is "Martes de
carnaval" in which she details a typical holiday fiesta. The
enthusiastic workers, who live together at a campsite located
on the hacienda, gather to consume huge quantities of roast
goat, rice, *chicha,* and *pisco.* When all have had their fill,
several men with guitars and strong voices enliven the
proceedings with fast waltzes and *marineras.* Almost as an
afterthought to the rich detailing of the scene, María Rosa
Macedo adds a slight episode about a young couple who plan
to elope during the course of the festivities. At best, however,
it is little more than a token gesture to plot and character
development.

"Algodoneros" is similarly long on local color and short on
attention to artistic and fictional considerations. It makes an
interesting contrast to the preceding story, because it depicts
the grueling labor and danger which are the peon's lot during
a regular work day. For the reader who wishes to know how
the daily tasks are assigned on a cotton plantation, the types of
labor performed, the tools used, and so on, this narrative can
be very instructive.

Finally, in "El desgraciau," the best story in the collection,
the author studies the more violent aspects of life on a sugar
hacienda. In so doing, she not only gives an excellent
portrayal of the boredom, the rivalries, the hatreds, and the
wild outbursts of peons who react in primitive fashion to the
problems and frustrations of life, but weaves a rather interesting plot as well around the themes of jealousy and revenge.

In *Hombres de tierra adentro,* a collection of stories which
was not published until 1948, María Rosa Macedo continues

to provide authentic regionalistic information about the inhabitants of rural Peru, particularly those who live on the coast.[28] Several of the selections, in fact, are similar to those found in her first book. "Carnaval," for example, has a setting very like that of "Martes de carnaval," describing the peons' humble, but lively, celebration of a fiesta. Of special note for folklorists is the description of a traditional dance called the Yunsa in which the couples move about a tree striking it with a hatchet until it falls. The author records the dance as follows:

"The Yunsa! The Yunsa!" they shouted. "Let's begin."

"Here we go," answered the musicians. And they struck up a lively tune:

> "Yunsita, yunsita
> Who will knock you down?
> Ha, ha."

Out came the participants who began to dance around the tree:

> "And the one who knocks you over
> will prop you up again.
> Ha, ha."

One couple left the circle, and the man wounded the silent, perhaps aching, tree trunk with the blows of his ax. Then the lyrics changed:

> "Dear little green willow
> who gives color to the beach.
> Lend me your shade
> until I go away."

The woman then took the ax and tried her hand at chopping. And so it went until the Yunsa began to waver. With a groan it toppled softly to one side. The peons became progressively happier as the party went on, and with the *pisco* flowing more and more freely, the embers of passion were stirred. (p. 26)

Obvious in the short stories of the foregoing authors is their attempt to portray aspects of the rich geographical and cultural diversity of Peru. It is equally apparent that the writers have been successful in their objective. Certainly, considering their works as a whole, the reader gains a broad and fascinating perspective of a wide range of rural peoples and regions. In this respect, of course, the writers who developed during the thirties are simply augmenting the work of the *Amauta* group. On the other hand, their greater devotion to plot and character development and their stronger emphasis on literary discipline (excepting Macedo) represents a definite advance. Diez-Canseco and Romero deserve special recognition for their craftsmanship. Following Palma, Valdelomar, López Albújar, and García Calderón, they deal skillfully with the technical considerations which govern the arrangement and presentation of narrative material.

Finally, there is another way in which the writers just studied differ from the *Amauta* group: their avoidance of tendentious social protest. This is not to say they lack social concern; however, they see the short story as something more than a forum for social reform. This is also not to say that social protest is completely absent from the stories of major authors during the thirties. As we will see in the next chapter, José María Arguedas and Ciro Alegría make protest a significant part of their narratives, but with a great deal more artistry and effectiveness than preceding writers.

## Writers of the Forties

All the major short story writers who come into prominence during the forties were born in rural areas of Peru. Their choice of these provincial birthplaces as backgrounds for many of their best works is a less coincidental but also common characteristic. Francisco Vegas Seminario frequently uses the Piura area as a setting for narratives in which he describes small town types and activities. Alfonso Peláez Bazán is fond of depicting the folkways of tiny farming communities in the Marañón river valley, and Francisco Izquierdo Ríos uses the quaint customs of isolated inhabitants in the jungle region around Saposoa. Finally, the sierra village of Huanta often appears as the background for Porfirio Meneses' tales.

Francisco Vegas Seminario was born in Piura in 1903 and completed his high school education in that city. He subsequently moved to Lima where, primarily at his parents' behest, he enrolled in the Facultad de Ciencias of the University of San Marcos. After an unsuccessful year, he was glad to leave school and return to Piura. In 1933 he obtained a job with the foreign service and was sent to the Peruvian consulate in Seville. A long and successful career as a diplomat followed during which Vegas held important posts in Bremen, Amsterdam, Berlin, Berne, Rome, Paris, and Caracas. In 1954 he returned to Peru and since then has resided in Lima where he devotes his time to writing.

Chronologically, Vegas should belong to the previous decade of writers; however, his literary career did not begin until 1946 with the appearance of *Chicha, sol y sangre,* a short story collection which won him immediate critical acclaim.[29] Indians, mestizos, doctors, priests, outlaws, and village gossips figure in stories set in the sierra or in the desert area of Piura. His most successful narratives are set against the latter background. He is especially talented at portraying small town life where the daily activities and customs are prosaic, but reassuring in their sameness—the *beatas* going to church in the morning, the men playing cards and arguing politics at night, the petty, monotonous gossip occasionally enlivened by a genuine bit of scandal, the faithful observance of holidays, and time-honored town protocol. These and numerous other details of local color are skillfully woven into the very fabric of the stories. His description of the provincial mentality is characterized by sharp insight, irony, and satire with much of the delightful humor deriving from his unflattering portrayal of the characters' foibles. At the same time, however, Vegas is obviously fond of those he exposes and identifies himself with them. This combination of sly ridicule and sympathetic understanding lends a special charm to "El enigma de don Juan Heredia," "Dos duelistas tras una mula," "El crimen de

don Faustino," and "Trabuco también tenía honor." In these
narratives, we meet such characters as Don Juan Heredia, the
town's most esteemed aristocrat and lover—in the very best
Spanish tradition—who becomes the subject of intense and
uproariously funny speculation when he suddenly ceases his
amorous activities. Another character is Ciro Cuello, a petty
municipal official whose whole life has been an exaggerated
dedication to duty and moderation until the day he decides
his honor has been impugned and a duel is necessary. Don
Faustino is an elderly man whose ideas about honor come
straight from the pages of a Calderonian *comedia*. This
attitude, plus the totally unfounded suspicions he has of his
wife, lead him into the most absurd of activities. Finally, there
is Toribio Fuentes, a proud and penniless parasite who lives in
constant fear that his rich and happy-go-lucky relative, Trabuco, will bring dishonor to the family name. In the first story,
which is an amusing treatment of the Don Juan theme, and in
the other three which are based on erroneous concepts of
honor, the marvelous incongruity and hence the humor stems
from the characters' overly serious appraisal of themselves and
their neighbors. Totally blind to the pettiness of their personal
activities, to the utter lack of meaning in what they consider
all-important, and to the essential humor in what they find
deadly serious, these heroes pompously and self-importantly
play out their roles. And yet, for all their painfully obvious
shortcomings, they are appealing to us; perhaps because we
recognize in them certain universal human weaknesses.

In other stories, Vegas treats the failings of his characters in
a serious manner. A striking example is "El primogénito de los
Godos" in which he brings his hero's concept of honor under
critical scrutiny. The plot is uncomplicated. Years before,
Fróilan Godos, son of a prominent hacienda owner, had
witnessed his father's murder at the hands of outlaws. As a
matter of family honor, Godos had tracked down and killed
all but one of the murderers. The action of the story is

primarily concerned with his search for and encounter with the last survivor, and the cruelty of his revenge is told in some detail. The author objectively depicts Godos' weaknesses along with his many attractive qualities. What may have begun as a quest for justice has perceptibly changed to the satisfaction of selfish, personal pride. The violence and hatred which inspired the hunt have become permanent qualities of Godos' personality. In the end, his cruelty, which has been hidden for awhile under a veneer of righteous indignation, is shown to exceed the cruelty of those he pursues in the name of honor. As in the stories where Vegas treats his characters' shortcomings in a humorous way, he leaves all value judgments to the discerning reader. His implicit question, however, is not lost to us: Is one justified in blindly admiring the fierce, personal righting of wrongs even though it is a distinctive, long standing Peruvian tradition?

In discussing his personal views on the craft of the short story, Vegas has stated that the all-important consideration is plot and that once having conceived it everything else falls into place naturally. [30] While we can readily agree that plot is an important aspect of his stories, it is also evident that he has taken a great deal of care with their style and structure as well. They have, in fact, much of the polish and perfection of García Calderón's tales. Nor is this similarity coincidental, for Vegas not only held García Calderón in high esteem, but was unmistakably influenced by him as well. The basic plot of "El despenador" is much like that of García Calderón's identically titled narrative. "Absolución de plomo" and "La momia del cacique" are strongly reminiscent of García Calderón's "¡Murió en su ley!" and "La momia." More important is the obvious similarity in the techniques used in writing these stories. This point is not made with the intention of downgrading Vegas' capabilities and originality, but rather to demonstrate his attention to the technical considerations of the craft of the short story and his careful observation of an acknowledged master of the genre. Though most of Vegas' production subsequent to *Chicha, sol y sangre* has been in the form of novels, he ranks, on the basis of this collection alone, as one of the outstanding writers of local color stories in Peru.

Alfonso Peláez Bazán was born in 1906 in Celendín, a village located in the Marañón river basin. He grew up on a small hacienda owned by his father and did not leave the area until it was time for him to begin his secondary education. He studied at a high school in Chiclayo, but before graduating was overcome by wanderlust and set out on an extended trip which took him through many of the villages along the Marañón. Finally tiring of this vagabond existence, he settled in Lima and completed his secondary education. After graduation, he returned permanently to the area of his birth where he divides his time between writing and teaching.

Though Peláez Bazán's interest in writing dates from his high school days, he did not begin his literary career until the late thirties; and it was not until 1946, with the publication of a book of short narratives entitled *Tierra mía* that he became well known. [31] That same year *Cuando recién se hace santo*, a collection of literary sketches of the Marañón region, was also published. [32] In addition, he has contributed stories and articles of a cultural nature to national newspapers and magazines.

The author uses the region of his birth as the setting for the majority of the stories of *Tierra mía*. He presents a wealth of local color material, describing in detail the way of life and beliefs of the people. He is especially fond of the humble owners of small farms and sympathetically depicts their religious practices, superstitions, and love for the soil. In "Los cuernos de la luna," he pictures a small valley where eight farm families live in isolation but in perfect harmony. The customs are simple and rigidly observed. Sickness is treated with special herbs and remedies passed from generation to generation; the crops are planted only during certain phases of the moon, with the Virgin always asked to bless them. The curious mixture of superstition and religion is seen during the dreaded dry season when the people alternate fervent prayers to the saints with reliance on the advice of a man purported to have magical powers. When tragedy, in the form of a flood, strikes the settlement, it is accepted stoically as God's will. This story and others like it in the collection are presented with a clear recognition of the characters' very narrow vision of life; but at the same time, the author implies a sympathy, even a nostalgia, for the essentially peaceful, comforting quality of an existence so firmly rooted in tradition.

Peláez Bazán adds to the picture of his charming and quaint native region by recalling some of the local legends. The stranger who questions or comments on one of the aspects of the area or about an inhabitant is used as a device to enter into this type of subject matter. The narrator then makes an explanation in the form of a tale. His story may be about a well-known local character, such as the deafmute who learned to speak the name of the girl he loved ("Maximo"), or about unusual animals. "Truhán" tells of a bedraggled old cur who for years has traveled by himself all over the area, never staying more than a few days in any one place, but always cheerfully welcomed by man and dog alike wherever he goes. Another example is "El toro bayo," the story of a wild and ferocious bull who in the years of his wanderings in the region has built a reputation of invincibility through his ability to avoid the traps of those who would seek to capture him. The material is not dramatic, but of just such happenings as these are the legends of isolated rural regions made. Because of his sensitivity and personal experience, Peláez Bazán is able to convey the material with a remarkable feeling of authenticity.

Unlike Vegas Seminario, Peláez Bazán has failed to combine his fascinating local color material with a careful, skillful approach to technical matters. Despite the relative shortness and simplicity of his narratives, they become monotonous in most cases during the course of the reading. This defect can be accounted for, at least in part, by the almost total absence of dialogue or monologue which could be used to vary the rhythm. Structural weaknesses and the overuse of certain narrative devices such as the formula with which he introduces the local legends are other drawbacks which detract from Peláez Bazán's short narratives.

Porfirio Menses was born in the small sierra town of Huanta in 1915. He spent his childhood in that area and grew up learning both Quechua and Spanish. In 1935, after some years of interrupted and disorganized studies, he completed his secondary education in Lima. He then returned to the region of his birth and for four years traveled around the small Indian villages as a singer. Certainly the authenticity and authoritative quality of his stories owe much to this unusual peregrination which served to acquaint him thoroughly with the Indians' life and customs. In 1940 Meneses returned to Lima to continue his education. He enrolled in the University of San Marcos, but left in 1947 without having earned a degree. Since then he has held positions as a history and dramatics teacher in high school and has directed a theatrical workshop for young people.

Meneses did not become seriously interested in writing until 1941 when José Diez-Canseco began to encourage his talents. He gained his first recognition by reading three of his unpublished short stories at a meeting of Insula, a literary club, in 1944. Like Vegas Seminario and Peláez Bazán, Meneses' first collection of short stories, *Cholerías,* was published in 1946 and established his reputation as a promising writer.[33] As the title indicates, these narratives are intended to picture some of the attitudes and customs of the Indian and mestizo world of the sierra. With few exceptions, the plots are simple. They are inspired by everyday situations in the sierra —a peon's discovery that he has been robbed, a family's pride in the bountiful corn crop, an old Indian's philosophical attitude toward his wife's unfaithfulness—which the author has observed and from which he has extracted the human interest by studying the characters' reactions. "Cosicha" and "Arrieros" are representative stories which treat the ever-present problem of theft in both an amusing and serious vein. The characters and their conduct tend to be stereotyped, but there is no doubt that such matters as the Indians' strong attachment to material possessions, and the matter-of-fact and implacable way they seek to restore that which is theirs, are faithfully drawn.

Of all the selections in *Cholerías*, "Contrabando" is outstanding because of its characterization and suspense. The plot is based on a common occurrence in the sierra—the brutal clash of two men in conflict—but the unusual, ironic circumstances surrounding their violent encounter set it apart from the rest of the stories. Meneses probes the mind first of one character and then of the other, while at the same time maintaining tension as the moment for their decisive meeting rapidly and inexorably approaches. One is a contrabandist who, in the night hours, cautiously makes his way along a precipitous mountain path with his load of smuggled goods. He is on his way to a nearby village where they will be sold, and his thoughts are on one thing—what he is going to do with the money he makes from the trip. While alert to possible dangers and firmly resolved to take the life of anyone who gets in his way, he feels no real fear. Having once made up his mind to take the risk, he accepts stoically the occupational hazards. Waiting in ambush at the edge of the village is a man who is also determined to kill if necessary. He makes his living by tracking down smugglers, a lonely and dangerous job at best. His adjustment has not been as matter-of-fact as the contrabandist's, for he is consumed with a violent hatred against those for whom he lies in wait. Perhaps the hatred has grown from the very nature of the job, that of waiting, always waiting, in the dark, lonely hours of the night. The position of the reader in this drama is a highly privileged one with an extensive knowledge and view into the action. He understands the psychic state of the characters better than they do themselves. He also knows a fact that is completely unknown to either of them—that they indeed will meet. The author alone, however, knows the outcome of the meeting, and he conceals it until the climax. At the same time as he is establishing the mental and emotional condition of the characters, Meneses keeps the reader continually and uneasily aware that the encounter is soon at hand. He does this by describing alternately the smuggler's difficult approach to the village and the ambusher's position of hiding, thereby focusing attention on the steady diminution of space and time. The final mute testimony of their violent encounter is two bodies, one riddled by bullets and the other punctured by knife wounds.

In summarizing the short stories of Meneses, we can say that he consistently is able to capture the unique local color of the region he is describing. His knowledge of the inhabitants makes him especially good at portraying his characters' reactions to different situations. He is less consistent in his attention to the finer points of the short story craft, though certainly not unaware of them as we have seen in "Contrabando." [34]

Francisco Izquierdo Ríos was born in 1910 in the jungle region around Saposoa. In 1926, after completing his secondary education there, he moved to Lima and enrolled in the Instituto Pedagógico. He graduated with a teaching certificate and had a choice of several positions in the capital, but decided to return to the jungle to take charge of a village school in the province of Moyobamba. Later he accepted a job as a secondary school inspector of the jungle provinces and was obliged to make numerous, difficult trips to outlying schools. In 1942 he returned to Lima to become the director of information for the Ministry of Education. Most recently he has been in charge of a night school in Callao.

Though Izquierdo Ríos' first work, a book of prose sketches and poetry, was published in 1939,[35] it was not until 1946 that he, like his contemporaries, came into literary prominence with the appearance of a collection of short stories entitled *Tierra del alba.*[36] In these narratives the author gives an interesting and accurate portrayal of the jungle region around Saposoa, including its physical characteristics and the mentality of its inhabitants. Environmental descriptions of the quaint villages and their lush, tropical surroundings are detailed, as is the presentation of the fascinating customs which abound in an isolated area just beginning to receive such conveniences as electric lights and radios. The characters—small merchants, farm families, teachers, petty government officials, itinerant salesmen, and vagabonds—are sketchily drawn and lacking in individuality; however, they are important as representative types of the region. An added element of authenticity is found in the liberal use of jungle terms and regionalisms. The reader who is not familiar with the environment and its linguistic peculiarities is apt to spend much of his time referring to an accompanying glossary.

Izquierdo Ríos' method of presenting local color is to give a lengthy introduction of setting and characters before entering into the plot of the story. If the setting is a village, he first details its appearance and then recounts its history and significance in the area. Next he introduces the inhabitants and their daily lives. We see the women congregating on special days to wash their clothes in the stream and the men, whose lives are closely linked to the soil, going to the fields. Carefully described are the occasional community parties, the only form of entertainment for these people of simple tastes. In some of the narratives, such as "Lindaura Castro" and "Bernacho," Izquierdo Ríos, like Peláez Bazán, relates local legends which add to the picture of a quaint, charming, isolated area with its roots deep in tradition.

Izquierdo Ríos is also capable of bitter social protest, though he limits it to only one story in the collection, "Juan Urquía," in which local color gives way to harsh commentary on the plight of the so-called *agregados,* the Indians who work on haciendas without just compensation. The plot is negligible as the author is mainly concerned with exposing a despicable feudalistic practice which exists in his region.

Izquierdo Ríos includes three stories from his first book in a second collection entitled *Selva y otros cuentos* (1949).[37] With one exception, the stories of his second collection are also intended primarily to present a colorful and authentic picture of a specific jungle region. The exception, "La maestra de la selva," is in one respect comparable to "Juan Urquía," since the author is again mainly concerned with exposing and protesting an unfortunate and unjust situation. This time it is the plight of the provincial school teacher who must work under the most adverse of conditions with little cooperation from her superiors and no understanding from the public.

Izquierdo Ríos' narratives are a significant addition to jungle fiction, but it should be noted that their depiction of the environment is different from that of the preceding works by Romero and Burga Freitas where it frequently appears as a hostile, powerful force or personality in conflict with the human intruder. While the jungle is amply described in Izquierdo Ríos' tales, it is never more than a physical setting for the activities of characters who are settled within their environment. The value of his stories is precisely in their fascinating and authoritative regional content. That the more technical aspects of the short story craft are not overly important to him is evidenced by the carelessly drawn characters, faulty narrative structure, and underdeveloped plots.

The four writers studied in this section are primarily concerned with delineating in a graphic manner the actual life of limited regions with which they are intimately acquainted.

None of them would pretend to have presented the whole truth about their particular area of interest; it is doubtful if this could ever be accomplished, however extensive and detailed their narrative collections might be. They have, however, captured representative aspects of the environments under consideration: physical settings, common customs, speech habits, superstitions, values, personal relationships, and the like. Sometimes these characteristics are presented with nostalgia; at other times they are given in a purely descriptive manner. They may also be described with irony, as in some of the delightful works of Vegas. If the merit of the stories produced by these men depended alone on their knowledge and insight into matters of local color, they certainly would rank very high. If we also consider the authors' artistry—for instance, their ability to combine regional material with proper devotion to plot and style—then only Vegas consistently hits the mark.

As we have seen, the majority of the short stories published during the late twenties, the thirties, and the forties are distinguished from those of previous periods by their marked regionalistic content. What is Peru? What is there about our heritage, our environment, our way of life that identifies us as a distinctive nation? What are our problems, strengths, and weaknesses? These and similar questions are the inspiration for narratives which, besides providing entertainment, perform a unique didactic function by informing domestic and foreign readers of the diversity of Peruvian landscape and culture and by noting some of the country's social ills. We have also seen that the fictional content and artistic value of the stories depend on the author's craftsmanship and his concept of the purpose of literature. Thus some of the works examined in this chapter provide an excellent combination of informative regional material, interesting plot, and effective

technique, while others bog down in local color detail or are
dominated by the particular "message" the author wishes to
convey.

The approach to basic technical problems by the authors of
this period does not differ fundamentally from that of their
predecessors. There are, however, some minor distinctions
that are worth noting briefly. First, as concerns the narrator's
point of view, we can generalize by saying that, like Valdelomar, López Albújar, and García Calderón, they use all the
various types of focus: first-person, first-person observer,
author-observer, and omniscient author. But of these narrative
viewpoints, they show a marked preference for that of the
omniscient author, a preference that can largely be explained
by the ready compatibility of such a focus of narration with
the descriptive and didactic materials they wish to present.

A highly significant, if limited, advance in the narrator's
point of view is made by Fernando Romero in a few stories of
the collection *Mar y playa* in which he is able to catch the
working of his hero's mind with a penetration and immediacy
not found in previous narratives and which, with the exception of some works by Ciro Alegría and José María Arguedas,
are not found until the narratives of the fifties. It is not that
preceding and contemporary writers failed to bring the reader
close to the thoughts and feelings of their characters; many of
the authors studied thus far did a commendable job in that
regard. They did not go beyond that, however, to re-create
what Leon Edel terms "the atmosphere of the mind." [38]

The most extensive example of Romero's technique is found
in "El nido extraño" where we enter the mind of a father,
Santos Paucha, who is brooding over the fact that his son, Juan,
has disappeared from home without leaving word:

After greeting you, I want to tell you . . . By Heavens! A guy
raises birds, and they turn around and pick out his eyes. Another
round, Don Rafo. The same thing for a change . . . My sons,
Paucha. Shut your ugly mouth, "Tamalazo." Your sons are a bunch

of easy marks. Are you going to try and compare any of them with Juanito? Now there's an intelligent boy . . . He took all the prizes at school this year. Didn't you know that?

Big plans . . . My future . . . But what did that ungrateful kid think he was doing? Didn't Santos Pauca have everything all planned? Who else but he was going to take charge of the guard post? My future . . . Good-for-nothing, cold-hearted. What am I going to tell Asunta? Don Rafo: Uncork a couple of bottles of your special wine. The special stuff, ah!

And the guard post in the northern zone? He was going to have to clean the rocks at Caleta Pelada all by himself. . . . Keep that carbine you gave me? . . . What for? Guns are for sissies who run away. . . . Right, Don Rafo? Right. More drinks, "Tamalazo." So you think your sons . . . Ah! Juan is more man than any of them. More man than all of them put together. The ungrateful kid. To pull out now during the nesting season—right when I need him most. Because the first pairs of *guanayes* and *piqueros* are building their nests in the ravines, Juan. They arrived yesterday. My future . . . I can't live at the guard post. What does the ungrateful kid want anyway? (p. 40)

This passage obviously does more than merely record an unspoken monologue. It catches the flow of the mind in all of its confusion, discontinuity, and mixture of relevancies and irrelevancies. Half-formed ideas, questions, exclamations of anger and disgust, snatches of imagined conversations, and fleeting memories of conversations which took place at other times fuse in a stream of thoughts that flow through the mind with a total disregard for chronology. In other words, the reader is confronted with the "direct mental experience" of the character.[39]

In regard to the use of dialogue within a story, the writers of this period generally follow the previous procedure of interspersing selected dialogues, that have the effect of dramatic scenes, with narrative passages. In some of their narratives, however, the dramatic scenes are less fully developed than those of previous writers; that is, they do not always have well-defined beginnings and endings, and the

conversational exchanges themselves, which tend to be elliptical, leave the answers to some questions, as well as the
questions to some answers, to reader inference. Diez-Canseco
and Fernando Romero both resort to this type of dramatic
particularity consistently. Diez-Canseco's technique is especially noteworthy. He uses a number of short dramatic scenes
in his stories and likes to begin the action, or start from a
transitional point in the action, with a dialogue. Since the
scenes are not given any lead-ins and the language of the
speakers is elliptical, the reader is occasionally dropped, as it
were, into the midst of an ongoing dramatic situation. The
scenes are short, and the subsequent narrative passages
quickly fill in details which cannot be inferred, so that the
alert reader is not confused or handicapped. Diez-Canseco's
skillful use of such dialogue scenes gives a special dramatic
vividness to his stories.

In a sense, all the authors of this period, with their serious
efforts to record authentically the peculiar speech habits of
their characters, attempt to characterize through dialogue.
However, since the characters are mostly representative types,
the characterization is usually of a general and superficial
nature. Some exceptions to this generalization can be found,
especially in the works of Diez-Canseco, Fernando Romero,
and Vegas Seminario, where some of the characters are
developed as individuals. These three authors understood, like
Valdelomar and López Albújar before them, that dialogue,
properly used, can have an important or even a major part in
presenting the psychological complexity of a character.

In previous references to the representation of vernacular
speech by the local color authors of this period, we have
touched on the problem of language usage—on the figures of speech, popular oaths, colorful imagery, and the
grammatical forms which are put into the mouths of the
characters. It should be emphasized that they go beyond a
simple reporting of popular and standard Peruvianisms; they

include vocabulary and linguistic patterns which are peculiar to limited social groups or particular regions. Fortunately, most authors include a glossary of the more obscure usages. Besides recording grammatical lapses and the rich variations in vocabulary, the writers also attempt to illustrate the different types of pronunciation by means of typographical indicators. The following passages by Macedo in *Ranchos de Caña* reproduce the typical speech of mulatto peons and are representative of the care that is generally taken by the local color authors of this period to reflect accurately the linguistic individuality of groups and locales.

—¿Qué tienes?
—Naa, mamita
—Tas casi blanca. ¿Te duele algo?
—La cintura, un poco.
—No hagas juerza y toma agua 'e cola 'e caballo.
—Güeno
—Yo tengo q' dir pa' la hacienda, a la cocina, que la Clemencia se ha enfermau.
—Ande nomás, mamá
—Ta luego pué. (pp. 53–54)

—Mira al "Palomito," dijo casi con ternura.
—¡Caray! Bien negrito, como su padre.
—Probe angel 'e Dió; capaz se quea huacho.
—¿Onde tá "Palomo"?
—En la champería. (p. 55)

["What's wrong with you?"
"Nothin' mama."
"You're almost white. Somethin' hurtin' you?"
"My stomach, a little bit."
"Well, don't strain yourself and go drink some horsetail water."
"Okay."
"I got to go up to the hacienda to work in the kitchen 'cause Clemencia's sick.
"Go ahead mama."
"So long."

"Just look at little Palomito," she said almost tenderly.
"He's goin' to be real black just like his father."

"Pore little angel; he could end up bein' a orphan."
"Where's big Paloma?"
"In the fields."]

Ornate and subtle forms of expression have little or no place in these stories and in this respect the vocabulary range has been narrowed. On the other hand, the presence of regionalisms, the names of innumerable flora and fauna, and the geographical terms associated with the various settings are significant additions to the vocabulary and have an important instructive function.

With the exception of Diez-Canseco, Fernando Romero, and Vegas Seminario, the local color authors are not as concerned with the matter of "single impression" as previous short story writers. When regionalistic or propagandistic material takes precedence over plot, it becomes less important to move the action rapidly forward to its climax and denouement and to eliminate all but the details which will heighten the desired impression. This does not mean, however, that the local color writers are blind to the basic narrative problem of economy. Their means of achieving economy are even the same as those of their predecessors in a few instances. A common device, for example, is the division of the narrative into numbered sections—like acts of a play—in order to make time skips without accounting for transitional details. On the other hand, their methods are sometimes just the opposite of those previously employed. Whereas earlier writers economized in descriptions of setting and character, the local color writers may economize with limited plot and action. Finally, they economize on occasion by using an elliptical style in their dialogues rather than by limiting the number and length of the dramatic scenes.

Our final technical consideration, the ordering of events, requires little comment. For the most part, the events of the stories follow each other in an ordinary chronological sequence, the only interruptions being made in the form of expository passages which provide background material. The two noteworthy exceptions are "El velorio" in which Diez-Canseco initiates the action at a point in time just prior to the denouement and then abruptly switches back to the genesis of the action to fill in the crucial details, and Fernando Romero's previously cited interior monologue where the normal passage of time is broken. It is not until the fifties, however, that Peruvian short story writers experiment extensively with brusque and illogical changes in the chronological pattern of their narratives.

# IV

## CIRO ALEGRIA AND
## JOSE MARIA ARGUEDAS
## PIVOTAL FIGURES

IT SEEMS CLEAR that Ciro Alegría and José María Arguedas are the two most significant and illustrious figures in present-day Peruvian fiction. Both are wholly products of the twentieth century, having come into prominence in the middle thirties with the publication of their excellent initial works, *La serpiente de oro* and *Agua* respectively. From that time until past mid-century, their literary careers have continued in ascendancy, and their talents are at present recognized by all who are familiar with Latin American culture. Because of constant reader demand, Alegría's principal works have been reprinted numerous times and some have appeared in translation. Arguedas' works, one of which recently won a Faulkner award, are also readily available.[1]

While the major writings of Alegría and Arguedas are widely known, the special position these two men hold within the history of modern Peruvian fiction is less well understood and appreciated. They can perhaps best be described as pivotal figures, for while sharing their contemporaries' concern for the national scene and its problems, they strive for and achieve new, more transcendent modes of expressing those realities. Their narratives are, in fact, a striking synthesis of that which has gone before and of their own innovations. Rural Peru, Indians and mestizos, local color, and social

114

protest are primary elements in their works; but these elements are consciously and masterfully blended with stylistic and linguistic techniques calculated to express as never before the complexities of character and environment. In this manner, Alegría and Arguedas, whose influence spans some three decades, form a significant link between the local colorists and the talented young writers of the fifties and sixties who also concentrate on form and technique as they seek new ways of expressing the essence of Peru.

Finally, it should be noted at this point that the popular reputations of Alegría and Arguedas are based primarily upon their novels. Although Arguedas has published two significant short story collections, he is best known for the excellence of his longer works. Alegría, who has had only one collection of short narratives published, is even less appreciated for his work in that genre—though, ironically, Alegría the novelist owes much to Alegría the short story writer, as we shall see. Because of the extraordinary skill of these two authors in the realm of the brief narrative, and because their stories possess, in fact, the same insights and depth of emotion as their novels, it seems especially important that these lesser known works be accorded proper attention.

### Ciro Alegría

Alegría was born in 1909 in the district of Sartimbamba of the province of Huamachucho near the Marañón river. He spent his youth on his grandfather's hacienda where he became thoroughly familiar with rural customs and with the Indians and mestizos of the region.[2] In 1926, after graduation from high school, he joined the staff of *El Norte*, a newspaper published under the auspices of APRA in Trujillo. The paper published not only his political articles but his poetry as well. He soon grew restless and a year later left *El Norte* to become a foreman on a road-building project and later a timekeeper for a bridge construction company. In 1930 Alegría returned

to Trujillo, enrolled in the university, and resumed writing for
*El Norte*. Within a short while, he abandoned both endeavors
and associated himself more closely with the *Aprista* organization. As a result of his political activities he was jailed in
Trujillo. In July of 1931 he escaped and tried to flee to
Ecuador, but was recaptured in the Marañón area and taken
to the penitentiary in Lima. He was released late in 1933 and
joined other literary men in founding the newspaper *La
Tribuna,* another important organ of APRA. Not long after-
ward, in 1934, he was forced to become a political exile from
Peru. He settled with his wife in Santiago de Chile where
they lived precariously on the irregular income he earned
from selling articles and short stories to Latin American
periodicals. Because of the combination of his uncertain
economic situation and the physical toll taken by his earlier
prison experience, Alegría fell ill. Fortunately, with the care of
his wife and friends, he quickly recovered and entered into
the period of his greatest literary production.

Alegría's first triumph was the publication of *La serpiente
de oro* in 1935, which won first prize in a contest sponsored by
the Nascimento publishing firm. In 1938, his second novel, *Los
perros hambrientos,* was awarded a prize by the Zig-Zag
publishing company. The high point of Alegría's career came
in 1941 when his novel *El mundo es ancho y ajeno* won first
prize in a contest sponsored by Farrar and Rhinehart Company and *Redbook Magazine.*[3] He traveled to New York to
receive his award at a banquet in his honor. John Dos Passos,
Waldo Frank, Gabriela Mistral, André Maurois, and other
figures of the literary world were present for the occasion.

Alegría remained in the United States during the war and
worked for a time with the Office of War Information. He also
taught at various universities and wrote extensively for such
periodicals as *Free World, Inter-American Monthly, Selec-
ciones,* and *América Latina.* After the war, he accepted an
invitation to teach at the University of Puerto Rico. Following

an extended stay there, he went to Cuba where he continued his journalistic and teaching activities. It should also be noted that he officially severed his *Aprista* ties in 1948. In 1957 Alegría briefly visited Peru after a twenty-three-year absence. He traveled through many parts of his native country and was enthusiastically received everywhere. He again took up residence in Cuba, but the pull of his homeland remained strong, and on January 15, 1960, Alegría returned to Peru, this time to stay. In 1963 he was elected to Congress and has since then been active both in political and cultural matters.

Perhaps the best way to begin our study of Alegría's use of the short story form is to recognize its presence within the general framework of his novels. On examining the unusual structures of these three prize-winning works, we find that it is possible to pick out a series of episodes which, though forming integral parts of the main narrative, could be considered and appreciated as stories in their own right. *La serpiente de oro*, for example, comprises nineteen chapters, each of which has its own unity. Naturally, these chapters, and for that matter all of the events of the novel, are linked together harmoniously so that they have an overall unity and interrelationship; nevertheless, considered individually, many of the episodes possess both the necessary independence, character development, and dramatic force to stand alone. One obvious example is the well-known incident of the astute "puma azul."[4] In this regard, it is interesting to note that the origin of *La serpiente de oro* was a short story, "La balsa," written by Alegría shortly after his arrival in Santiago. It was rejected by *La Crítica*, an Argentine newspaper, because it was too long to fit their format and it remained unpublished until the author expanded the idea into its present form, with the original episode contained in one chapter.

The structure of *Los perros hambrientos* shows further interesting relationships between the short and long narrative forms. Intercalated at strategic points of the novel are five folktales told by two characters. Again, though the tales are specifically and skillfully designed to further the main action of the narrative, they could be extracted from its framework and read individually without loss of meaning.[5]

Finally, *El mundo es ancho y ajeno,* which was inspired in part by one of the incidents in *Los perros hambrientos,* contains several portions which have the attributes of independent short narratives, particularly those episodes in the section following the destruction of the Indian community of Rumi: the tragedy of Amadeo Illas and his wife, Calixto Paucar's sad experience in the mines, and the adventures of Augusto Maqui in the jungle. In addition, a few folktales similar to those of *Los perros hambrientos* are interpolated within the novel.[6]

Algería's regular short stories are neither numerous nor very well-known. For many years his stories remained unpublished or dispersed in anthologies and in the literary sections of Latin American newspapers. In fact, it was not until 1963, with the appearance of *Duelo de caballeros* that any of his stories became available in collected form.[7] The collection is quite complete and has been highly acclaimed in Peru; but unfortunately, it was published in such a limited edition that it failed to attract much attention outside of the country. The majority of Alegría's short stories have a rural setting and within this general classification can be subdivided as follows: stories with an Andean setting and principally Indian characters, stories with an Andean setting and mestizo characters, and stories with a jungle setting and white and mestizo characters. He has also written narratives with urban settings and with humble city dwellers as the main characters. Finally, his legendary tales, which he has especially adapted for children, can be considered as a separate category.[8]

Alegría's profound understanding of his humble characters and their environment comes through as strongly in his short narratives as it does in his novels. This is particularly true in

his stories of the sierra in which he studies the psychology of
the Indians, capturing their beliefs, values, and special view of
nature with a sensitivity not found in previous Indianist
fiction. "La piedra y la cruz," for example, gives an authentic
portrayal of their unique religious customs which have, over
the centuries, become a curious mixture of Catholicism and
deeply ingrained pagan practices. The title itself is appropri-
ately symbolic of the confusion: the stone as a prime expression of ancient Inca devotion in juxtaposition with the cross as
the most revered sign of Christian worship. The surface events
of the narrative are slight. A young boy, son of a hacienda
owner, and his faithful old Indian servant are traveling by
horseback high in the Andes. They are approaching the
location of an ancient and revered wooden cross that is
surrounded by piles of stones. For years—nobody knows
exactly when the practice started—travelers in this lonely
place, particularly the Indians, have carried a stone to the
cross as an act of worship. The old Indian stops to gather
stones along the way. Though the boy tells him not to pick up
one for him since the custom is only for ignorant Indians, he
does so anyway. He then spends the rest of the journey urging
the lad to observe the ritual also. He even predicts dire
misfortunes if the boy refuses and cites cases he knows of
personally where those who neglected the sacred observance
have suffered tragedy. For the old Indian, this act of
veneration has dual significance. It represents his sincere effort
to placate the two religious forces—Catholicism and ancestral
paganism—which have become inextricably fused in his mind.
At last, they reach the site and, in that moment of silence on
the cold, wind-swept peak, the boy, overcome by the solitary
majesty of the surroundings and the simple faith of his
companion, also offers a *piedra votiva.*

Undoubtedly, Alegría's most difficult and noteworthy accomplishment in this charming tale is his portrayal of the
Indian's animistic vision of nature. He recreates that complex

perception of natural surroundings, in part through dialogue which is simple in content but profound in its revelation of the old Indian's intimate relationship to his environment. The following conversation between boy and Indian shows perfectly the latter's cult of the stone as an intuitive concept that he feels deeply though he has difficulty in formulating it:

"It's okay to place lamps and candles before crucifixes or statues of saints—but stones!"

"Why it's all the same thing, little *patrón*. A stone is devotion too."

The Indian remained thoughtful for awhile and then making a special effort to express his ideas adequately, he said slowly: "Look here, little *patrón*. A stone is not a thing that you take lightly. What would become of the world without stone? It would collapse. Stone sustains the earth. Just like it sustains life." [*] [9]

Alegría's perceptive descriptions of landscape are also a means of giving special insight into the Indian's animistic sensibility. In short passages which show his mastery of language and his propensity to experiment with unusual word images, he captures the very essence of the Andes—solitude, vastness, cosmic mystery. It is the essence experienced by the Indian who feels himself intimately and harmoniously linked with his natural surroundings, with a world in which all objects are possessed of life and movement. The subtle, suggestive function of Alegría's descriptions is clearly evident in the following passage where he uses the verb to animate, in fact, almost humanize the imposing landscape. The italics are mine.

De pronto, ya no hubo siquiera arbustos ni cactos. La roca *se dio a crecer* más y más, *ampliándose* en lajas cárdenas y plomizas, tendidas como planos inclinados hacia la altura, *alzándose* verticalmente en peñas prietas que remedaban inmensos escalones; *contorsionándose* en picachos aristados que *herían* el cielo tenso; *desperdigándose* en pedrones que parecían bohíos, vistos a distancia; *superponiéndose* en muros de un gigantesco cerco del

[*] For original Spanish passages, see pages 173 ff.

infinito. . . . La roca viva *surgía* hacia un lado, *agrupándose* hacia las nubes, y por el otro *descendía formando* un abismo. (pp. 76 and 113)

[Suddenly there were no more bushes or cactuses about. The rock *began to loom* larger and larger, *extending* itself in violet and lead-colored slabs whose smooth surfaces stretched toward the heavens. It *rose* vertically into black cliffs which gave the appearance of huge stair steps, *twisted* itself into sharp peaks that *wounded* the tense sky, *scattered* itself in immense boulders which resembled huts in the distance, and *superposed* itself into walls of a gigantic, endless fence. . . . The live rock *surged* to one side, *crowding* upward toward the clouds; it *came down* the other side, forming an abyss.]

If Alegría provides a unique insight into the Indian mind, he also understands and is able to convey convincingly certain aspects of the mestizo mentality, especially their strong sense of dignity and justice. A good example is "Calixto Garmendia," a story set in a small Andean village. Calixto, the hero, is a conscientious and ambitious carpenter who, through hard, honest work, has become the owner of a house and a small plot of ground at the edge of the village. Because he has achieved a measure of economic independence and because of his intense personal pride, Calixto refuses to curry favor with the local dignitaries. His stubbornly held ideas of justice frequently cause him to help the Indians and poor whites of the area when it would be safer to mind his own business. During the course of the narrative, Calixto is seen in three ways: first, as a man respected by the common people because of his economic accomplishments and his moral rectitude; second, as a man combating through legal means the unjust confiscation of his property by those who resent his independence and courage; and third, as a man embittered and disillusioned by his country's corruption, but still uncompromising in the fight for his beliefs. As in *El mundo es ancho y ajeno*, the conflict of idealism and realism is a basic theme; that is, the ideal of a country in which justice and dignity for all who merit them is contrasted with the sad reality of a country in which many deserving citizens do not enjoy these rights. For the author, Calixto Garmendia is an ideal hero: courageous, intelligent, and hardworking. In a broader sense, he is representative of the mestizo class which Alegría feels will someday realize its goals and desires with hard work and perseverance. The important thing is not that Calixto fails in his valiant efforts to obtain justice, but that he has the spiritual and economic resources to wage that struggle well. Once this is understood, the story, which at first seems to be an exercise in pessimism, takes on a new dimension of meaning. Above all, Alegría is practical in his assessments of his country's shortcomings and in his solutions for them. Peru has both a high ideal and a less desirable reality; the ideal can be achieved only if citizens with the necessary desire and capabilities will assert themselves with wisdom and steadfastness. Alegría states this very thesis succinctly in an essay written earlier in New York. His words on that occasion throw important light on the intent of this story:

Within this problem, the mestizo plays a key role, since he forms a vital link between tradition and a new way of life. Maintaining, as he does, old values and at the same time being in a position to take advantage of the educational and economic advantages necessary for his emancipation, he appears on the Latin American scene, tacitly or explicitly, as one who has come to claim what is rightly his. (*Novelas completas*, p. 334)

During his youth, Alegría frequently used to accompany his father on cattle-buying trips which took them over very rugged parts of the sierra. Those journeys served to acquaint him not only with the ever-present danger in such remote areas, but also with many of the Indians who regularly traveled the narrow and risky Andean trails. "El cuarzo," a story set on a lonely mountain trail, is obviously inspired by his youthful experiences. He captures a tragic, decisive moment in the life of an anonymous Indian who is making his way along a treacherous path that leads from the mine where he is employed to the hut where his wife and child live. Only brief mention is made of the other characters, as the author centers exclusively on the character of the traveler and his circumstances. Alegría presents his narrative as an omniscient author, but, much of the time, the point of view is that of the Indian, whose thoughts both establish his character and provide a view of the action. At the start of the trip, the Indian is happy; he has his earnings, a pretty piece of quartz for his child, and the anticipation of rejoining his family. The author introduces the first jarring note by abruptly switching the point of view from the pleasant introspection of the Indian to a description of his natural surroundings. Flashes of lightning cross the sky, and the first hailstones began to fall. An electrical storm accompanied by hail is one of the most dreaded hazards of the sierra. From this point in the story Alegría alternates between the Indian's increasingly troubled and chaotic thoughts and the increasing fury of the storm which is beginning to produce landslide activity. It is not that he fears for himself; he is worried rather about the safety of his family. Suspense is developed effectively by playing on the alternating hopes and fears of the reader, who views the conflicting thoughts which pass through the traveler's mind. He is deeply troubled, but he consoles himself with the thought that he has carefully chosen the location of his hut in order to avoid the danger of such storms; he becomes almost frantic, however, as the storm grows in intensity. At the moment of maximum tension, which is also the end of the story, the Indian reaches his hut and finds it buried under an avalanche.

Technically, this is one of Alegría's most effective short stories. He chooses to present the character as he lives for a few, brief moments; but it is a vital, defining fragment of life during which we are able alternately to hope and suffer with the character in such a way that we come to know him as a person, though we know neither his name nor his background. The economy of words is extraordinary, as is the strongly sustained suspense and the subtle use of implication and suggestion. Every narrative detail, including the descriptions of nature, is designed to develop character and promote the rapid forward motion of the action. It is, in a word, an excellent example of modern craftsmanship in the short story form.

"Muerte del cabo Cheo López" is another noteworthy example of Alegría's short story technique. The setting for this narrative, unlike the majority of his works, is the city. Despite the change of environment, however, he continues to focus his attention on the less privileged classes, the main character in this story being a day laborer. Though the main purpose of the story is, like that of "El cuarzo," to present the psychological reaction of the main character to a tragic experience, the technique is more complex. Stripping the story of all expository narration, Alegría limits the viewpoint strictly to the words of the anonymous hero who tells of the death of his friend to a listener, Don Pedro. Since Don Pedro does not answer, the story is, in effect, a monologue in which the hero reveals his psychic state and at the same time advances the action. It is interesting to note that though the monologue is being spoken aloud, its fluidity and confusion of half-formed ideas produce much the same effect as an interior monologue designed to show the chaotic flow of the mind. In other words, the nature of the main character's speech gives special insight into the state or atmosphere of his mind:

Pardon me, Don Pedro . . . I know that this is surely not a proper way to come to you . . . But I want to tell you . . . How can I explain it to you? . . . Eusebio López has died . . . I know that you don't know him, and very few people did know him . . . Who's going to pay any attention to a poor man who lives in a shack? . . . That's why I didn't go after the bricks . . . We were friends. Do you understand what I mean? (p. 71)

Grief has robbed the speaker of coherence. With complete disregard for chronology, his attention, now especially susceptible to association, switches back and forth between the present and past experiences:

That odor! You understand Don Pedro . . . It smelled that way in the Pacific . . . It's the smell of dead men, Japanese . . . Dead men are all the same . . . The thing was that out there we were advancing . . . our dead and wounded were picked up, and we found Japanese who had been dead for days, rotting away . . . Now Cheo López has begun to smell like that . . . (pp. 71–72)

Plot is, of course, almost nonexistent, explanatory details are absent, and the viewpoint is uniquely limited. Nevertheless, if we participate, as it were, in the creative process of the story, responding to the author's subtle direction, we not only receive an unusual insight into character but are able to supply to our own satisfaction the background material which is unexpressed or vaguely hinted at.

Alegría, who has dealt with the jungle area in his novels, also uses this setting for one of his early short stories, "La madre." It relates a young man's first day as a rubber camp worker. His initial task is to accompany Don Floro, an old man hardened by years of adversity in the region, on a hunting trip in order to supply fresh meat for the camp. Don Floro explains that they will try to bag some young monkeys which are delicious to eat once one becomes accustomed to their resemblance to babies. The young man shudders inwardly but determines to harden himself to jungle life, even as the old man has. Don Floro shoots and wounds a female monkey who falls to the ground still clutching to her breast a terrified baby. When she fixes them with a hurt, reproachful stare, the young man forgets his brave resolve and bursts into tears.

This story, which likely has some autobiographical basis, can readily be classified as a story of initiation.[10] The plot is uncomplicated but suited to the main purpose of presenting the hero's painful adjustment to a new environment and a different standard of conduct. Alegría does not fall into the obvious trap of exaggerated sentimentality, and yet it is fair to state that his handling of the theme betrays an inconsistency and immaturity not found in the other stories studied here. Along with these faults, it has some virtues, not the least of which are the descriptive passages, notable for their unusualness and for the exactness of meaning they lend to the scene. The following line, for example, describes the fatigued rubber workers as they appear during their leisure time in the jungle. The general feeling of boredom and tiredness is strikingly captured: "they would go out in the clearing and spread their arms like tired birds in the sunlight." A veteran of the jungle, who has been so long in the region that he has seemingly absorbed some of the environmental qualities which surround him, is described in these words: "He was a husky sexagenarian with jaguar-like eyes and a tangled, dirty beard. His pale skin had taken on the greenish-yellow coloring of the jungle, and his gray beard resembled a handful of the liana which hangs from tree trunks." [11]

Finally, Alegría's stories for children should be mentioned. As has been pointed out, they are adapted from legends. ("El sapo y el urubu" is based on a legendary theme found in most cultures, "El castillo de Maese Falco" is a Colombian legend, and "La leyenda del nopal" is an Aztec tradition.) They have neither the originality nor the technical excellence of his other short narratives; however, their ingenuous style admirably captures the authentic spirit of the folktale as it has been passed down orally from generation to generation. And Alegría has, of course, a profound knowledge and feeling for popular tradition. In his novels, as we have seen, he is fond of inserting folktales which are told to an appreciative audience by Indian cuenteros skilled in the art of storytelling. In his stories for children, Alegría himself assumes the role of a cuentero and delights his juvenile audience.

Alegría brings to his short stories the same qualities that are present in his novels: a unique and understanding portrayal of his characters' customs and psychology that transcends mere local color, a sincere concern for social justice that is not marred by exaggerated protest or sectarianism, and highly successful stylistic innovations. To these attributes, common to both his long works and short works, he adds a special aptitude for the technical demands peculiar to the short story form. It is hoped that someday soon his stories will be published in an edition more readily available outside of Peru, for while they are not well known, they are a fundamental part of his fiction production.

### José María Arguedas

Arguedas was born in 1911 in the Andean town of Anda-huaylas and lived his formative years among the Indians in that area of the sierra. After the death of his mother, when he was three years old, he lived in the neighboring village of San Juan de Lucanas which later served as a setting for several of his narratives. There he experienced many privations and adversities; but he also enjoyed pleasant moments participating in the Indians' festivals, learning their songs, and listening to their folktales. Since his father, a lawyer, had to spend much of the time traveling, Arguedas was frequently left in the care of others and was even taken in at one time as a long-term guest of an Indian community. Quechua, the principal language of the Andean Indians, became a part of him, as the sound of it was in his ears and on his lips throughout his childhood and youth. He completed his secondary schooling in Huancayo and Ica; in 1929 he moved to Lima where he enrolled in the University of San Marcos. Almost immediately, he became active in intellectual circles, collaborating with Augusto Tamayo Vargas, Alberto Tauro, and other prominent young men of the period in the editing of a periodical called *Palabra*. Despite the change to more cosmopolitan surroundings, he did not lose his interest and affection for his childhood environment and for the humble people who had shared with him so generously. In addition to his efforts to improve educational opportunities for Indians,[12] he made scholarly investigations of their folklore which have been recognized as invaluable contributions to Peruvian culture.[13] Subsequently he accepted a job in the Intitute of Ethnological Studies of the National Museum of History. At present he is head of this institute as well as being a professor of literature and folklore at the University of San Marcos.

Though Arguedas was strongly interested in fictional writing from his youth, he hesitated to give literary expression to his unique view of the Quechua world because he lacked confidence in his creative abilities. At the same time, he was disturbed by the inadequate portrayal of Indian character by those compatriots who could only visualize this humble inhabitant of the sierra as a stereotype. Finally, impelled to depict these people as he knew them to be, Arguedas wrote *Agua* (1935), a volume of short stories which was his first attempt at fiction. It was followed by: *Yawar fiesta* (1941), a novel; *Diamantes y pedernales* (1954), a book that contains the narratives from *Agua* plus other stories; his prize-winning novel *Los ríos profundos* (1958); and *El sexto* (1961), a novel.[14] Most of these works are set in the sierra, and though whites and mestizos appear in them—sometimes prominently —the author's principal concern is always the Indian.

The short narratives contained in the two collections, *Agua* and *Diamantes y pedernales,* are characterized, as are his novels, by a unique understanding of Quechua mentality and tradition that distinguishes them from other Indianist fiction, including even the very perceptive works of Alegría. Arguedas presents the Indians' customs, values, personal feelings toward nature, tender affection for animals, and frustration in the face of the social evils which victimize them. He has the personal conviction and involvement of one who not only knows but also identifies himself with those feelings. The distinctive insight Arguedas gives into the Quechua's vision of the world is due as much to his ingenious use of language as to his comprehension of the subject matter. He has created for his Indian characters a mode of verbal communication so personally expressive that we are able to perceive life, in many of its aspects, through their eyes. In realizing this linguistic innovation, he went through an interesting and trying process. He initially wrote "Agua," title story of his first volume of narratives, in correct, literary Spanish. The result was completely unsatisfactory to him, since it rang as false as many of the works which he had branded as inadequate expressions of Indian reality. He describes his feelings as follows:

I wrote the first story in my best and most "literary" Spanish. Later, I read it to some of my Limeñan friends, and they praised it. But I developed a growing hatred for those pages. No, neither the people, the village, nor the landscape resembled in the slightest that which I was attempting to portray—one could almost say that which I wished to proclaim! With a language that was essentially false, I had depicted an equally false, invented world —a world without marrow and blood; a typically "literary" world in which the words had consumed the work. Meanwhile, in my memory, in my very being, the true theme continued to burn, untouched. I wrote the story over again and I understood perfectly as I did it that traditional literary Spanish was going to be of no use to me.[15]

But if Arguedas knew that a literary Spanish was not the answer, he also was certain that Quechua would not serve as an alternative because it was understood by so few. How then was he to convey authentically the Indians' mentality and manner of speaking in a language not their own? After painstaking experimentation, he reached a solution: a special language based on fundamental Spanish words incorporated into Quechua syntax. He employed the new idiom to his satisfaction in rewriting "Agua" and in the composition of the other selections contained in his first volume of stories. It has, in fact, been the basis of his distinctive style in all subsequent narratives. In order to achieve maximum effectiveness from this unusual form of expression Arguedas employs monologue and dialogue to a large extent. The result is startling. For the first time we begin fully to realize that though we may have previously been supplied with rare insights of the Indians' attitude toward their tradition and present day reality, we have never before shared so completely their inner thoughts and their vision of the white man, the village, the landscape, the animals, and other Indians. In other words, the Indian has seemed largely "inscrutable" because our vision has been largely external. In the following monologue from "Agua," in which the speaker complains about the unjust actions of the rich landowners, we see an example of Arguedas' exceptional linguistic experiment. There is an obvious but unexaggerated simplicity in both syntax and content which gives the words such authenticity that we feel ourselves witnesses to the sincere, personal feelings of the speaker:

Los indios son buenos. Se ayudan entre ellos y se quieren. Todos miran con ojos dulces a los animales de todos; se alegran cuando en las chacritas de los comuneros se mecen, verdecitos y fuertes, los trigales y los maizales. ¿Por culpa de quién hay peleas y bullas en Ak'ola? Por causa de don Ciprián nomás. Al principal le gusta que peleen los ak'olas con los lukanas, los lukanas con los utek' y con los andamarkas. Compra a los mestizos de los pueblos con dos o tres vaquitas y con aguardiente, para que emperren a los comuneros. Principal es malo, más que Satanás; la plata nomás busca; por la plata nomás tiene carabina, revólver, zurriagos, mayordomos, concertados; por eso nomás va al extranguero. Por la plata mata, hace llorar a los viejitos de todos los pueblos; se emperra; mira como demonio, ensucia sus ojos con la mala rabia; llora también por la plata nomás. ¿Dónde, dónde estará el alma de los principales? (p. 150)

[Indians are good people. They help each other and they love each other. They look tenderly upon everyone's animals; they are happy when the wheat and maize—green and healthy—wave gently in the communal fields. Who is to blame for the quarrels and trouble in Ak'ola? Why it's Don Ciprián's fault. The white master likes it when the Ak'olas fight with the Lukanas, the Lukanas with the Utek' and with the Andamarkas. He bribes the mestizos in the villages with two or three little cows or with brandy so they will harm the communal Indians. The white master is bad; worse than Satan. He is only interested in getting money; to get money he has rifles, revolvers, whips, overseers, peons; he even goes to strange lands to get money. For money he kills, he makes the poor little old men of the village cry, he treats us like dogs. He looks like a devil; his eyes become dirty with evil rage; he cries only because of money. Where, oh where, can the souls of the white masters be?]

Unusual effects are created by the short, sometimes abrupt, phraseology as brief sentences are interspersed with longer ones containing several thoughts. The thoughts themselves, though coming in rapid succession, fall into logical patterns. The mode of expression is thus uncomplicated without in any way being an exaggerated sort of pidgin Spanish; thus, while capturing the speaker's essential simplicity of character, his dignity and native intelligence are preserved. The same characteristics can be noted in the following dialogue from "Agua":

—Así blanco está la chacrita de los pobres de Tile, de Saño y de todas partes. La rabia de don Braulio es causante, Taytacha no hace nada niño Ernesto.
—Verdad. El maíz de don Braulio, de don Antonio, de doña Juana está gordo, verdecito está, hasta barro hay en el suelo. ¿Y de los comuneros? Seco, agachadito, umpu (endeble); casi no se mueve ya ni con el viento.
—¡Don Braulio es ladrón, niño!
—Más todavía que el atok' (zorro). (pp. 105–6)

["The little fields of the poor people of Tile, of Saño, and everywhere are withering away like this. The rage of Don Braulio is causing it; *Taytacha* (Indian god) isn't helping us a bit, little Ernesto."
"True. The maize of Don Braulio, Don Antonio, and Doña Juana

is fat and healthy; it's green, and the soil is even damp. And the
maize of the communal Indians? It is dry, scrawny, feeble; it
scarcely moves any more in the wind."
   "Don Braulio is a thief, child!"
   "Even a bigger thief than the fox."]

It is interesting to note that the distinctive rhythm and style
of this idiom carries over into the brief narrative passages as
well. Carefully interspersed among dialogue and monologue,
they are designed to underscore the meaning and emotion of
the characters' observations. The following passage, which like
the language of the Indians is simple and yet lyrically
expressive, captures the melancholy and coldness of the
sierra:

Pantacha levantó su corneta y empezó a tocar una tonada de las
punas. De vez en cuando no más Pantacha se acordaba de sus
tonadas de Wanakupampa. Por las noches en su choza, hacía llorar
en su corneta la música de los comuneros que viven en las altas
llanuras. En el silencio de la oscuridad esas tonadas llegaban a los
oídos, como los vientos fríos que corretean en los pajonales; las
mujercitas paraban de conversar y escuchaban calladas la música
de la puna. (p. 105)

[Pantacha raised his horn and began to play a highland melody.
From time to time, Pantacha remembered his own melodies of
Wanakupampa. At night, in his hut, he would make his cornet cry
with the music of the communal Indians who live on the high
plains. In the silent darkness those melodies reached our ears like
the cold winds which race through fields of grass. The little
women would stop conversing and listen silently to the music of
the puna.]

Arguedas has succeeded in creating a language that intimately expresses the Indians' attitudes and beliefs and at the
same time preserves necessary universality by being under-
standable to all readers of Spanish.[16] With the aid of this
unusual style, he is able to portray with sensitivity the Indians'
complex relationship to their natural surroundings. He has, in
a sense, recreated their animistic world in which natural and

supernatural elements blend harmoniously, and anything from
a mountain to a flower is potentially capable of thought, will,
and action. The mountain peaks, for example, are frequently
the subject of contemplation and conversation among the
Indians. Sometimes a mountain inspires fear and respect: "I
reached the foot of the mill; I climbed the highest wall and
looked from there at the head of 'Chawala,' the blackish, erect
mountain that threatened to fall on the alfalfa fields of the
hacienda. He frightened us at night; the Indians never looked
at him after dark. And on clear nights, they always conversed
with their backs to that mountain" (p. 182). Occasionally, the
Indians compare the size and temperament of the various
peaks, referring to their expressions of kindness, anger, impa-
tience, and tranquility. From time to time, an Indian gives vent
to his exasperation at the seeming impotence of a mountain in
which he has placed his faith. Even the venerable Tayta Ak'chi
who watches over a village and has the power to move about
at night is not spared such insults: "Ak'chi is a nobody in
Ak'ola. . . . He becomes annoyed in vain; his lordly airs mean
nothing. He accomplishes nothing in that region; he is only
useful as a stopping place for clouds" (p. 155).

The rivers and streams are also possessed of life and special
meaning for the Indians: "Mariano had grown up under the
protective care of a small river" (p. 16). Along their courses,
they carry messages meant for the Indians' ears; they may
even supply melodies for Indian musicians:

On the night of the 23rd of June those harpists would follow the
path of the little streams which cascade into the deep river—the
main river that flows out to the coast. There, under the great
waterfalls which fall in torrents over the black rocks, the harpists
would "listen." On that night only, the water composes new
melodies as it strikes the rocks and sweeps along its channel! Each
harpist has his own special waterfall. He stretches out, face
downward, hidden under the overhanging rocks. . . . Some of
them cling to trees above the ravine where the sobbing torrent of
water flows swiftly. The following day, and during all of the yearly

fiestas, each harpist plays melodies which have never before been heard. The river dictates this new music directly to their hearts. (p. 24)

The sun is also perceived as more than a natural object. In the story "Agua," Ernesto, the narrator, blames the bright rays of the sun for the shortage of water in San Juan: "Tayta Inti [the sun] surely must have wanted the earth to die; he stared at it directly with all his might. His wrath made the earth burn and men cry" (p. 118). Here, the sun is personified, becoming in the process almost a projection of the cruel hacienda owner who is further adding to the Indians' plight by cutting off their precious water supply. On other occasions, however, Tayta Inti is benevolent and comforting. In the following passage from "Los escoleros," the sun is seen initiating and sustaining a feeling of contentment and harmony which links man, beast, and the land in an intimate relationship:

The sun shone brightly in the clear sky; its white light, which tenderly warmed my body, spread out over the ravine and over the distant mountains. . . . The sparrow hawks fought playfully in the air; the *pichiuchas* screeched happily over the little mountains of *taya* and *sunchu*. Everything seemed content. The singing headwaters of the Jatunkocha—from which the people of Ak'ola drank—cascaded over the black rocks. (p. 149)

There is, in fact, a curious sort of equilibrium implicit in the Indians' total view of the natural world. While perceiving clearly both the positive and dissonant elements of their surroundings, they also see an essential harmony that supports them and with which they are anxious to enter into relationship. Thus, the sun that dries and withers on occasion also gives joy and warmth; the supernatural objects of worship which pose a threat are counterbalanced by those that protect and give guidance; the existence of animals that do damage is mitigated by the presence of other animals whose principal function seems to be that of overcoming them. Snakes, for example, are a potential hazard for the Indian farmer, but nature has also provided the *chaucato*, a bird that alerts him when the antagonists are in the area:

The *chaucato* sees the snake and denounces its presence. Its lyrical voice breaks with excitement. When it discovers a poisonous snake, it screeches, but more as a warning than from fright. And other *chaucatos* fly excitedly to the place of discovery. After alighting nearby, they hop about the ground pretending to be frightened and making a terrible racket as they call to each other. The peasants rush quickly to the spot, seek out the reptile, and kill it with blows from their machetes. (p. 71)

But there is an even more profound, inclusive harmony that Arguedas' Indian is able to perceive in nature under ideal conditions. It is a harmony that links nature in its totality, transcending the barriers of time and space and bringing into unique, unexpected contact diverse and widely separated elements. The following passage from "Diamantes y pedernales" is a moving revelation of this special vision:

In no other place on earth do things fuse as they do in that light. The radiance of the stars reaches down to the very depths, into the soul of things, to the essence of the mountains and rivers. It touches the color of the animals and flowers; it enters the human spirit. And everything is united in that resplendent, crystalline silence. Distance disappears. Man gallops along, but the stars sing in his soul and glow in his hands. Heaven and earth become one. (p. 40)

In this curiously animistic world where everything is possessed of life and where man, animal, the soil, and the elements are closely associated, the Indians frequently feel a special tenderness toward their surroundings. Their love of the soil is seen in their sheer joy at observing a healthy plant or a field ready to yield a bountiful harvest. They are grieved by the sight of unhealthy and dying crops, be it their own or their neighbors'. Nature, in fact, has a distinct power over the Indians' state of mind. Thus their feelings frequently reflect

the very same feelings expressed in nature and nature's
creatures: "The freshness of the morning, the happiness of the
mother ravine consoled me anew" (p. 149). An invisible, but
vital, interpenetrating bond of emotion is sometimes seen to
possess the Indian and all he observes to such a degree that
each seems to share a common psychic state in which the
distinction between man, animal, and object blurs perceptibly: "I was confident and brave this morning. . . . The
haughtiness of Tayta Ak'chi, the happiness of the young colts
and the little mountains, the proud flight of the hawks and
sparrow hawks warmed my blood and made me bold" (pp.
145–46).

The animals of the sierra serve not only as objects of
affection but frequently as emotional supports for the Indian
who readily shares his joy and grief with them. The timid,
delicate vicuña has a special significance, since in his seemingly fearful, lonely existence he mirrors and shares a similar
aspect of the Indian's experience: "Out on the cold plains
. . . the little vicuñas cry, looking mournfully at the travelers
who pass along the road. The Indians have a special sympathy
for this animal; they love it. Their troubled eyes light up with
tenderness when they see it there on the white capped
mountains of the *puna* and as they listen to its sad, small
voice" (p. 158).

In "Los escoleros," a cow called Gringa is the pride and joy
of the whole Indian community. Though the animal is the
property of a widow, it is, in terms of affection and concern,
owned by all the Indian village. The children in particular
love it: "in her mouth with its thick lips, in her limpid blue
eyes, in her little ears, we found an expression of kindness that
melted our hearts. Gringacha! . . . I loved her like a mother"
(p. 136). They suffer when the cruel hacienda owner casts
covetous eyes on Gringa, and when he kills the cow in a fit of
rage, they feel a tragic loss: "Mama, Gringacha! I threw
myself on her white neck and cried. . . . The warmth of her

body, her smell of fresh milk, faded away little by little, along with my happiness" (p. 176).

The feelings that Arguedas' Indian has for the animals he loves and appreciates are complex, representing something more than mere affection. He visualizes a unique relationship whereby the distinction between human being and animal is absent to the point that they can share emotions and aspirations. Nowhere is this better illustrated than in the story "Diamantes y pedernales," where the Indians speak of Mariano, the harpist, and his pet sparrow hawk as having the same soul:

The sparrow hawk watched him knowingly. The musician's face was reflected brightly in the deep eyes of the sparrow hawk. Mariano played a carnival war dance and then pranced about with great leaps, not once taking his eyes off the sharp-beaked little bird. "They're friends! They understand each other! They surely share the same soul!" exclaimed Antolín, observing that during those moments of rejoicing Mariano and the sparrow hawk did not cease to look at each other. "The heart of the 'Upa' [Mariano] is beating as if it were that of the sparrow hawk." (p. 21)

Arguedas makes social protest a vital factor in his portrayal of the Quechua world. Rebelling at the injustices which the Indians have had to suffer, he vigorously exposes and criticizes the oppressors. In commenting on *Agua*, he states that the exposition of the tragedy of the present day Indian reality in Peru is one of his major aims. It is an aim that has been evident in all of his fictional works:

*Agua* was written, to be sure, with hate, with the fury of pure hatred; a hatred that is born of universal love, there in that region of the world where two hostile bands confront each other with cruelty.

The stories in *Agua* contain the life of an Andean village in Peru, a village in which the struggle between the two traditional factions is clearly and obviously delineated. Only two classes of people exist there, each representing an essentially different world: the large landholder, completely convinced by the evidence of centuries of his innate superiority over the Indians; and the Indians who have zealously preserved their cultural unity precisely because of the fanatical and cruel force to which they have been subjected. (p. 5)

In voicing his protest, Arguedas does not use irony or satire. The force and conviction of his presentation derive from his personal involvement. He empathizes with the victims of a society that seems bent on degrading them physically and morally. It is a society where cruel landowners exploit the Indians, using them as virtual slave labor, encroaching on their communities, killing their animals, depriving them of their water rights, and enslaving the children to pay off a father's debt. It is a society in which the victim has no real recourse to law and where his pleas are largely ignored even by those who claim to look after his best interests. It is, finally, a society in which any attempts at active or passive resistance by the victims are brutally suppressed.

"Agua," the title story of his first collection of narratives, is a good example. It deals with the Indians' sad plight because of the lack of water. The fields are withering and their children are starving. Don Braulio, a drunken, morally corrupt hacienda owner whose word is law in the area, controls the water supply and does not allow them their rightful turn to irrigate their small plots of ground. The situation finally becomes so intolerable that the younger Indians try to seize the water supply by force. Their pitiful, unorganized resistance fails, and many of them are brutally shot down. It should be noted that the unhappy outcome is clearly foreseen at the start. The older and more resigned members of the community, although desperate and frustrated, fail to give any support to the young ones. They know that such protests are hopeless, and this note of hopelessness dominates not only their outlook but also the atmosphere of the narrative.

The same mood dominates "Los escoleros." Don Ciprián, another ruthless *terrateniente*, rules the area and torments the

Indians. One of his favorite tactics is to round up their cattle at night and declare that the animals have strayed onto his land, and, therefore, must be given up as forfeit. All protests are futile, and the oppressed resign themselves to suffer the cruelty and humiliation which seems to be their lot in life.

Arguedas' Indians react to their social environment with the same sensitivity as they do to their natural surroundings. That is, they are keenly aware of both positive and dissonant elements and they strive to make their lives as harmonious as possible within this framework. Wrapped up in their tradition are the concepts of compassion, sympathy, and cooperation. When they are encroached upon by a society that contains just the opposite characteristics, they become confused, weak, and sometimes even as corrupt as their corruptors. Or to put it another way, they begin to lose their true identity in the cruel, hostile, social environment. Arguedas expresses this viewpoint repeatedly, but nowhere is it more clearly expressed than in "Los escoleros." Only when the ruthless Don Ciprián—who comes to symbolize not only a class of oppressors, but a corruptive society as well—is absent from the area can the Indians be themselves. During those happy intervals they are able to shake off their lethargy, confusion, and servility as they respond with joy and release to the love of Doña Josefa who, in turn, is representative of an ideal, harmonious society:

Doña Josefa strummed vigorously on her guitar; the peons and the other women clapped and gave encouragement to the couple dancing. Without need of brandy or corn beer, Doña Josefa knew how to make us dance and be happy. The peons were not furtive around her; they were not silent and stupid-acting as they were when the white master was present. They showed her their true hearts, their simple, loving hearts. (p. 159)

It should be noted that Arguedas advocates no concrete social, political, or economic reforms to aid the Indians. In fact, he registers a clear vote of no-confidence to the long list of superficial solutions proposed by the church and by political parties of his country. At the same time, however, he does more than simply decry the social evils that victimize the indigenous population of present day Peru. Evident in all of his work is the purposeful establishment of the dignity and worth of the Indians as human beings whose special heritage and sensitivity stand as rich, untapped resources for the nation. Implicit, as well, is the admonition that this broader foundation of understanding and appreciation must first be firmly laid if specific programs for meeting the Indians' immediate needs are to be successful.

In summary, the literary production of Ciro Alegría and José María Arguedas marks them as the two most significant Peruvian writers of the last three decades. This significance does not stem from their choice of themes, characters, and settings, because they, like the majority of the writers up until the fifties, continued to produce an authentically national narrative with emphasis on the rural area. The great triumph of Alegría and Arguedas is rather the result of their vision. First, due to experiences of childhood and adolescence and the subsequent serious observations of their adult years, they are able to bring to their works an intimate knowledge of the region and the people. Second, in their concern for the problems and aspirations of the common man in Peru, they have been able to avoid exaggeration or narrow sectarianism. Their presentations of these matters are sober, impressive, and convincing. Third, both authors are master craftsmen who pay careful attention to style. Alegría's expressive metaphors and imagery and his depiction of nature reflect a masterful command of the language. Nobody before or since Arguedas has given such authenticity to the Indians' mode of expression. The happy synthesis of these three factors in the works of Alegría and Arguedas is one of the most remarkable phenomena in Peruvian literature.

# V

## NEW DIRECTIONS
## SINCE 1950

It is difficult to make definitive statements about many of the short story writers who have emerged since 1950. They are promising, but their careers are incomplete; and in a land where few can afford to devote themselves full-time to creative writing it is not unusual for a fine, active beginning to be followed by sporadic production, or even complete silence. One thing is certain, however. The new generation of writers is reacting strongly against the long and restrictive dominance of the regional story. The young authors, while not completely forsaking rural Peru, turn with increasing and marked awareness to other settings and characters. Thus, the city becomes a focal point for many of the stories with the social, economic, and psychological problems of urban dwellers—rich and poor alike—providing a creative stimulus. The misery of slum inhabitants is exposed, at times with an unmistakable note of social protest. The psychological stresses and strains of the white collar worker seeking economic solvency, the painful experiences of individuals who belong to emerging middle groups seeking to establish their own social patterns, or the boredom of young socialites are described and evaluated. In short, we find in this new group of writers an awareness and a preoccupation with the general socioeconomic ferment which has become so characteristic of major Latin American cities since World War II.

But if these young writers have turned their attention to the city, they have not entirely neglected rural Peru. The sierra, in particular, continues to form the background for many stories. In a few of these, local color remains a dominant factor. In others, however, psychological analysis of character, reassessment of tradition and traditional values, and a tendency toward an unconventional treatment of *costumbrista* elements have replaced the more customary presentation.

It should be noted that these writers have, to a much greater degree than those of preceding periods, achieved a balance between national and international concerns. Thus, whether detailing urban or rural Peru, they are fully cognizant that on a more universal level they are also dealing with certain moral and spiritual problems common to modern man. The rejection or loss of tradition and the frantic quest for new values on the Peruvian scene are understood to be a reflection of modern civilization. Likewise, the confusion, misery, and desperation which dominate contemporary Peruvian society are seen as but one example of a complex moral and spiritual bankruptcy that is universal. In other words, while presenting the problems of their own country, they escape narrow localism through their understanding of and identification with the distressing and precarious existence of all mankind.

The writers who have emerged since 1950 also give evidence of an increased concern for principles of the art of modern fiction. This is seen in the frequent and skillful use of such technical devices as internal monologue, flashback, and cinematic effects, plus linguistic experimentation to find idiomatic formulas which fit the special world of their characters. The influence of Joyce, Faulkner, Hemingway, and Dos Passos is especially noticeable. Most of the young writers are thoroughly conversant with the works of modern and contemporary authors of Europe and the United States. An example is

Carlos Zavaleta, one of the most promising of the group, who has made several excellent studies of Faulkner and Hemingway. As for national authors who have exercised unquestionable influence, Ciro Alegría and José María Arguedas stand out as forerunners of the current intense linguistic preoccupation.

The authors who portray the urban scene with the greatest insight are Enrique Congrains Martín, Julio Ribeyro, and Sebastián Salazar Bondy. Congrains, born in Lima in 1932, is a restless and unusual personality who has worked at a wide variety of jobs including those of teacher and shoe salesman. His works are in some respects reminiscent of Erskine Caldwell and John Steinbeck, and he is the first to admit their influence on his writings. Believing firmly that literature should serve a social as well as an artistic purpose, he documents his works by living within the environment and closely observing the characters he treats. Several of Congrains' stories and novelettes have appeared in *La novela peruana*, a publication of the Círculo de Novelistas Peruanos, an organization that he helped form to encourage young Peruvian writers. In addition, he has published two collections of short narratives, *Lima, hora cero* and *Kikuyo*.[1] In many of these stories the slums of Lima, particularly the peripheral *barriadas*, provide the setting.[2]

"Lima, hora cero," the story from which his first book takes its title, gives a realistic and detailed picture of this blighted area. Briefly stated, it concerns the inhabitants of a slum community struggling to survive under impossible conditions and their desperation at being dispossessed of the property on which they have settled. Although the author uses interesting narrative techniques, the story's main value is its documentary accuracy. With all the authority of a sociological case study, the narrative portrays the beginnings of a *barriada*, its development and social order, the type of people who live there, and how they survive. We learn, for example, that due to the lack of running water, *barriada* dwellers must purchase this necessity in nearby areas of the city. Each week different persons are assigned the task of supplying water for the community, which must cooperate in order to preserve its miserable existence. We also learn that these people know how to entertain themselves. They organize weekly parties and even hold their own beauty contests. But in addition to giving such interesting facts as these, Congrains succeeds in making his characters human beings who cannot always help their miserable circumstances and who, instead of being despised as immoral, problem-creating elements of society, must be helped to rehabilitate themselves. While objectively portraying both the faults and virtues of the *barriada* dwellers, he wants to make society realize its responsibility to deal immediately with a social and economic problem that is fast reaching explosive proportions.

In the same collection, Congrains has a story, "Cuatro pisos, mil esperanzas," which depicts other urban problems— the chaos that has resulted from the rapid change in class structure and the steady growth of industrialization, the resulting upheaval of human relationships and responsibilities, and the frantic search for new values and identities. Congrains describes a complex of new apartment buildings designed to accommodate families of white collar workers with modest incomes. Rather than concentrating on one family, the author chooses many families. These newly settled apartment dwellers have basic problems and aspirations ironically identical. They have the same frustrated dream that their move to the modern structures will somehow bring true contentment to their drab lives, the same nagging worries about money, the same petty desires to stay in the boss's good graces and perhaps receive a minor wage increase, the same confusion and consternation about their proper social level, the same rootlessness and lack of ties with the past with no stability in the present or confidence in the future. In short, they each make the same pitiful effort to be happy in a shallow, meaningless existence.

Now, brothers, it's time to relax. All day long we have been slaving behind our desks: papers, memorandums, orders, invoices. But enough of that now! Life is like the color of the walls and buildings: optimistic, nothing but optimistic colors. Pleasant colors: yellow, orange, green, blue, cream, pink, sky blue. The person who planned these buildings carefully avoided the use of gray, maroon, or gloomy lead colors. One could even say that we live in an ivory tower. Here we are not surrounded by tin cans, cardboard boxes, rotting wood, mud, adobe, straw mats, or excrement. We are well off, brothers; our children can grow up in their marvelous ivory tower. And we, contented, can die a bit at a time—a bit here in Matute and a bit there behind our desks. And why not? Considering these colors, these tones, our biweekly salaries, our meals which are neither good nor bad, our mediocre happiness, our petty problems, our affectionate and happy wives, our radios and our movies, our parties and occasional drinking sprees, and our children who will one day imitate us—considering everything that makes up our lives, it is certainly fitting to count ourselves fortunate and to delude ourselves a bit. We are happy! We are men! * (p. 140–41)

But the new dwellings are a false refuge to which they flee in vain, because they cannot flee from what they are personally. Congrains pities these people as victims of the psychological and social dislocation which inevitably accompanies the great changes currently sweeping over Latin American society. They are part of an emerging middle class that gropes desperately to find a place within a society in violent flux. On the other hand, he despises them for their lack of vision, their petty concern for personal comforts, their absurd failure to appreciate the real plight of their poverty-stricken brothers which they witness every day. He captures the situation in all of its irony in a conversation between an apartment dweller and her daughter. The conversation is repeated with minor

* For original Spanish passages, see pages 176 ff.

variations at key intervals in the story, thus underscoring a basic theme:

"Mama, doesn't that little old lady who tends the chickens get cold at night?"
"I don't know . . . and besides, what difference does it make if she does get cold?" (p. 145)

"Mama, doesn't the little old lady who tends the chickens get hungry?"
"I don't know child . . . but after all, what do we care if she does get hungry?" (p. 148)

"Mama, what if the little old lady's children don't have any toys?"
"Look here, child, don't think about such foolish matters. Those kids don't even know what toys are. They can play with anything —little stones, tin cans, old boards, baby chicks. Don't worry yourself child, they have their own kind of toys." (p. 149)

Julio Ribeyro was born in Lima in 1929. He is a graduate of Catholic University and has traveled extensively in Europe. *Los gallinazos sin plumas*, his first and best known collection of short stories, contains several selections with the city as background.[3] The protagonists of all these stories are the poverty-stricken day laborers, servants, and beggars in Lima. Despite this emphasis, there is, in general, less social preoccupation in his stories than in those of Congrains. All of the narratives in this collection are realistic, but the most strikingly so is the title story, "Los gallinazos sin plumas." In this, his most widely acclaimed tale, Ribeyro creates a moving portrayal of the daily tragedy of the urban pariahs. Again, the setting for the action is a *barriada*. The protagonists, or rather the victims, are two little boys who live with their old grandfather. The grandfather keeps a pig that he is attempting to fatten; early each morning he sends the two lads to scavenge in a garbage dump for scraps of food for the animal and, incidentally, for themselves also. The meaning of the title is made shockingly clear when the boys compete with the buzzards for the choice morsels of the filthy, germ-infested area. The grandfather's total disregard for his grandchildren and for human life in general is contrasted grotesquely with his almost paternal care for the voracious pig whose every want is attended. He is a man brutalized by a lifetime of physical and spiritual deprivation. The daily contest for survival by the boys is seen as one of those unbelievable, absurd tragedies where a new generation of human beings is early starting on a process that also will finally destroy their spark of humanity. Ribeyro is not squeamish in his presentation of the tragedy and in his description of the squalid surroundings. The basic plot details are, in fact, so appalling that in the hands of a lesser writer, the narrative could easily have been so exaggerated as to be unconvincing. Ribeyro succeeds both in shocking and persuading by his matter-of-fact, almost casual revelation of these details. He does not protest, lecture, or decry. He simply gives the reader what could be called a slice of the life of the slum dwellers of Lima and, in so doing, he is able to strip away the impersonal mask that tends to obscure the individual tragedy of large scale poverty in the city.

Sebastián Salazar Bondy was born in Lima in 1924. Like both Congrains and Ribeyro, he is concerned with the current problems of the city dweller; but, to a greater degree than either of his contemporaries, he is also preoccupied with the philosophical implications of modern man's existence. Salazar was a graduate of San Marcos, traveled extensively abroad, and had an active career as a journalist until his death in 1965. In addition to his newspaper activities, Salazar also wrote plays, poetry, and essays, and published a collection of short stories called *Náufragos y sobrevivientes*,[4] a work of penetrating insight into the lives of city dwellers, rich and poor alike. He makes acute observations, not without a certain tinge of irony, of such persons as the young socialite, who leads a pointless and selfish life of idleness, or the unmarried couple of the city's swank social register who cynically resort to abortion in order to avoid scandal. In stories whose tone is faintly but unmistakably sad and pessimistic, he may examine the psychological and spiritual gulf that exists between people on different levels of society or lament the inevitable untimeliness of death, as well as the lonely, impersonal quality of its occurrence within the crowded, bustling, frantic urban setting. Though all the stories have clearly designated Limeñan backgrounds, they could just as well have taken place in any other city. For what Salazar is mainly concerned with is a world in which values have been distorted, goodness has been corrupted, honesty has been diluted by hypocrisy, and happiness has become unattainable. In a general sense then, it is accurate to say that he shares in the so-called existentialist mood.

His best story from a technical point of view, and also one that effectively reflects Salazar's concerns, is "Volver al pasado." It details the return of a young woman from the provinces to Lima, the place of her birth and childhood. The narrative opens with her going to visit the former family home. Salazar relies on flashbacks to give the reader just sufficient background information to appreciate the implications of the visit. Interestingly enough, the flashbacks are within the mind of the protagonist as she recalls childhood scenes. Thus, the present action unfolds in the form of straight narration and dialogue, while the past is simultaneously revealed through occasional, interspersed glimpses of the girl's thoughts. A sleepy-eyed woman answers the door and, after first refusing the girl entrance, finally allows her to step inside. The reader as well as the protagonist is confused by the woman's evasive answers and seeming unwillingness to allow her the satisfaction of looking through the home of her childhood. Then, in a totally unexpected ending, both reader and girl are appalled when the woman reveals that the place is now a house of prostitution and everyone's daytime sleep is being disturbed by the intrusion. The narrative is technically excellent; especially effective is the abrupt ending which climaxes a carefully sustained and developed interest. Also, it has a special shock quality because of the incongruity of the events. The author has shown us a world in which innocence, nostalgia, and bright anticipation—personified by the girl— are brushed by cynicism and evil. The result of this contact— which, by implication, is continually and under many and varied circumstances taking place within society—is a sad and irrevocable damage to the positive qualities of life.

Not all of the urban stories written since 1950 reflect the themes just discussed. There are a few, with the city as a background, which could better be classified as fantastic. Julio Ribeyro, in particular, has written some fine imaginative tales which are contained in *Cuentos de circunstancias.*[5] Some of the selections are hauntingly serious in tone, reflecting the influence of Kafka; in others, high good humor dominates. In all of the stories, Ribeyro uses highly imaginative settings and events to provide a unique interpretation of ordinary human experience.

Rubén Sueldo Guevara has written one of the finest stories of this type of fantastic fiction in recent years, "El fugitivo."[6] The author is a young man whose literary production has been limited thus far to newspaper and magazine publications. "El fugitivo" is a striking narrative in which all elements are skillfully and functionally related. It is told in straight narrative form, but the full significance of the tale is not revealed until the very end. The reader, therefore, is expected to take an active part in the story as it develops. Indeed, this is exactly what we do as we attempt to understand what is happening at successive stages of the narrative.

At the beginning, a man is fleeing from an unknown danger as he races breathlessly toward his own familiar neighborhood. The reader assumes that he is being pursued by an enemy who is taking advantage of the deserted streets and the

dark night. The mystery deepens, however, when the unknown pursuer disappears, and the man finds himself alone
among the destroyed houses and buildings of his neighborhood. Still looking for rational explanations to fit the scant and
ambiguous information, we might conclude that the protagonist
is the victim of an earthquake or similar catastrophe and, in
his fright, has momentarily lost his self-control and equilibrium. The fantastic element of the story assumes greater
importance with the reappearance of the dread pursuer, this
time described in such a way that it seems to be something
supernatural. The protagonist is chased through the streets,
caught, and pushed down from behind. The next morning the
man's body is found, and we are suddenly returned to reality
when an onlooker remarks how strange it is that the very hit-
and-run driver whom the police have been seeking is found
dead at the scene of the original accident, apparently also the
victim of a hit-and-run driver. Sueldo Guevara keeps the
reader guessing throughout the story as to whether he is in a
world of fantasy or reality. The scene is always shrouded in
mystery, yet rational explanations are possible. As the story
develops, the situation becomes increasingly fantastic until the
very last words when the implications of the action are
abruptly revealed. The story is a masterful mixture of fantasy
and reality which is perfectly sustained to the end.

While the current writers do not entirely neglect rural Peru,
most of those who continue the tradition present local color distinct from that of the immediately preceding decades. Two fine
interpreters of the rural scene are Carlos Zavaleta and Eleodoro
Vargas Vicuña, though neither limits himself exclusively to this
type of narrative. Zavaleta, who was born in Huaraz in 1928, is
a graduate of San Marcos and has done advanced study in the
United States. Besides scholarly publications, he is the author
of some excellent short stories, his most significant work thus
far being a collection entitled *La batalla*.[7] His special approach to regionalism is particularly interesting in the title

story of the collection. The setting is a small Andean village on the day of the *condor rachi* festival, a dangerous and exciting event in which a giant condor is tied between stakes with only its head allowed to move freely while contestants take turns striking it with their bare fists as they ride by on horseback. The unwary or uninitiated can easily lose an eye, an ear, or a finger. The spectacle is seen through the eyes of a young visitor who acts as an interpreter of the action. It is important to note, however, that this curious rural custom is not presented in the prosaic sense of providing an interesting piece of regional information. With Zavaleta's unconventional approach to the *condor rachi*, it ceases to be a colorful, traditional festival, becoming instead a grotesque orgy with surrealistic overtones. The author plays up the bestial aspects of the spectacle, and we observe the change taking place in the participants who, under the stimuli of alcohol and imminent danger, are gradually degraded to a level even below that of the ferocious bird of prey they are torturing. This is particularly evident in Chueca, one of the richest and most powerful men in the region, whose participation in the fiesta is witnessed with great admiration by all the local inhabitants:

The Indians and the drunks became frightened when they saw that Chueca had taken his rein and was savagely whipping the condor. Standing in its shadow, shielded from the sun, he viciously lashed the bird amidst curses and the spattering of blood. . . . A half-hour later the condor was still alive. Its talons were free, its beak stained with blood, and the accursed red pool which grew larger on the ground around it was licked and kissed by the dogs. The more corn beer Chueca drank, the faster and harder he whipped. Then, leaning from his saddle, he grasped the bird's leg in a flash, and maddened by the strength of its bones and the unsuspected metallic hardness of its flesh, he yanked with all his might. The Indians stood off to one side, the guitars were silent, and there was Chueca, drunk, falling off his mount while at the same time shouting curses and frothing at the mouth. Then he attacked the condor again, grabbing at its feet and feathers, and with the bonds suddenly broken, man and bird fell struggling together on the ground. But that still did not mark the end. The executioner got to his feet and sank his boots in the bird's breast, drinking a sea of blood. Finally losing his balance, he fell next to the panting condor who glared at him and squawked feebly. Its wings were now motionless; only its talons moved weakly as the blows fell. And the savage, drunken man continued to talk to the ground and to the scattered feathers, cursing the almost lifeless carcass of the bird and striking the Indians who tried to get him to stand up. (pp. 24–25)

In its absolute violence, the scene takes on a quality of unreality, and we are no longer witnesses of a time-honored tradition, but of a strange and repellent event. A subtle analysis is made of the young visitor who comes to the festival compelled by some overpowering inner force. It is as if he had regressed from another plane of civilization to participate for a time in the activities of this people. When he leaves, that which had attracted him for the moment seems strangely incongruous, and he cannot decide whether to admire or abhor the people and their strange custom.

In comparing Zavaleta's treatment of Peruvian tradition in this and similar stories with that of preceding writers, the difference is both striking and obvious. Whereas the local colorists from the late twenties through the forties were primarily concerned with finding a national identity through a search for customs and values typical and peculiar to the various rural regions, Zavaleta is challenging the worth and meaning of those very traditions in the contemporary scene. He is asking what values should be discarded as outmoded or unworthy and what traditions should be maintained because they preserve a true Peruvian identity. What aspects of the heritage, even though distressing, must be recognized and adjusted to because they cannot be erased or avoided? These are questions similar to those asked by Hemingway and Faulkner.[8] And it is not surprising that the similarity should exist since Zavaleta has studied these men with special care. But they are questions which sooner or later must be asked anyway by a sensitive young man such as Zavaleta, a young man from the provinces who has grown up close to tradition, but who has traveled and read widely, whose worldview is sophisticated, who is acutely aware of the vast cultural, social, and economic changes which have swept over his country since World War II. He is a young man who loves his country, but at the same time feels the necessity to re-evaluate its past in relation to the present.

Vargas Vicuña was born in Arequipa in 1924. He has worked at a variety of jobs including three months as a miner at Cerro de Pasco. He is an assiduous contributor to national newspapers and magazines and has in recent years taken an interest in drama production in Lima. His short stories are collected in two books, *Nahuín* and *Taita Cristo*.[9] Most of these narratives take place in the sierra, but the author has little interest in the exterior aspects of Andean life. He is mainly concerned with the psychological reactions of his characters to unusual and bizarre situations. We observe, for example, a child's thoughts and actions during a wake and a man's spiritual deterioration after a tragic flash flood. Technically, Vargas Vicuña's narratives are unusual. In all his stories, the reader must participate and respond to the author's subtle suggestions. The narratives are all related in the first person with heavy reliance on monologue or dialogue. In most cases the scenes are isolated, seemingly clipped from the surroundings, and are given to us without benefit of background information. Thus, while striving to analyze the implications of the protagonists' words and actions, the reader often absorbs only a series of impressions until the very close of the story, which is shocking in its sudden revelations. Illustrative of this procedure is "En la altura" (*Nahuín*), the story of a young Indian who comes upon a man and woman embracing in a field. He apparently knows them and is shocked by what he has seen. From that point on, the narrative is primarily an interior monologue with the reader solely dependent on the

protagonist's troubled and chaotic thoughts. We assume, as
the young man makes his way to the hut of the girl's father,
that he is in love with her and that she has been unfaithful to
him. The assumption is correct, but we are spared the
complete and shocking truth until the very last words when it
is revealed that the other person involved is the girl's brother.

Due to a lack of perspective, it is impossible, of course, to
make more than general and qualified evaluations of the
present group of short story writers. Nevertheless, we may list
Zavaleta, Congrains, Salazar Bondy, Ribeyro, and Vargas
Vicuña as authors who have already established solid literary
reputations. All things remaining equal, it also seems reasona-
ble to predict that within this group Zavaleta and Ribeyro,
because of their versatility and imagination, should eventually
rank high on the list of Latin American authors as maturity
and experience add to their unquestionable talents. Sueldo
Guevara, whose "El fugitivo" we have discussed, is also a
promising writer of both rural and fantastic narratives.
Unfortunately he has published only a limited number of
works in local periodicals. If his literary production increases,
he too could be added to the list.

Other young writers not to be overlooked are José Durand,
José Bonilla Amado, Raúl Galdo Pagaza, Luis Alberto Ratto,
José Miguel Oviedo, and Mario Vargas Llosa. Durand, whose
earlier publication was limited to scholarly works, has begun
writing short stories in the last few years. So far, he has
interested himself solely in psychological and fantastic narratives. Bonilla and Galdo have written both rural and urban
stories. They are realists in the style of Congrains, and an
unmistakable note of social protest is present in several of
their works. Ratto writes stories of the city, and his emphasis
is on psychological studies. Oviedo and Vargas have written
both rural and urban stories. They also are primarily interested in the psychological impact of modernization and
urbanization on their country. The production of these six is

very limited thus far. Though they display real talent, it is too early to make any predictions about their literary futures.

The concept these young writers have of the modern short story form is basically the same as that of their predecessors; however, in their handling of three of the five problems confronting every writer of fiction they make alterations and advances which are worth noting briefly. The most apparent change is seen in their language usage. On one level, the change is obvious, reflecting simply the treatment of new subject matter and a modification in emphasis. Naturally, the presentation of current urban problems, settings, and characters means the introduction of many new words. It is a vocabulary further enriched by post–World War II technical terms which have become a part of popular parlance. Even in those stories that treat rural matters, the break with the preceding local colorists is easy to discern. Gone are the numerous regional terms, popular local expressions, and carefully recorded speech peculiarities of a given group or area. But beyond those easy-to-see differences in usage, there is a more subtle, less easily explainable linguistic preoccupation that reflects a basic change of attitude toward the function of language within a story. Whereas the local colorists were primarily concerned with giving an authentic view of the external and the collective, the writers of the fifties and sixties, like Alegría and Arguedas, try to achieve a more complex mode of expression, one that provides through its symbolism, special metaphors, similes, and other rhetorical devices a deeper understanding of their characters' values, problems, and relationship to environment.

A further reflection of these authors' desire to present a unique, more meaningful insight into the characters in their stories is seen in the distinctive handling of another basic technical consideration, the narrator's point of view. It is safe to say that, like their predecessors, they use all the fundamental types of focus; however, what distinguishes them is their

predilection for turning inward on their characters' mental
experiences in order to present the human psyche in all its
complexity. Thus, for the first time in the history of Peruvian
fiction, we witness an extensive use of interior monologue.
Earlier, of course, we noted Fernando Romero's limited but
effective utilization of this technique; previously Alegría and
Arguedas had also experimented successfully with this
method when they wished to capture, in a special way, the
psychic life of their heroes. But the consistent and widespread
employment of this means of describing the movement and
the privacy of consciousness is more properly a characteristic
of the writers of the fifties and sixties.

Examples of both direct and indirect interior monologue [10]
can be found in the short stories of these writers. Luis Alberto
Ratto makes striking use of direct interior monologue in
"Humo," a narrative in which he strictly limits the reader to a
first-person view of the fluid and chaotic states of consciousness of a man who has committed a terrible crime. As
we can see from the following passage which is dominated by
incoherence, the author's intent is to capture a psychic state
and only incidentally does he impart information:

Don't blow smoke in my face! I used to stun butterflies that way.
They would fold their wings and go to sleep. Here he is now with
the incense! And I, quite the little altar boy, trying not to step on
my cassock. I prefer to ring the bell, father. They have just
opened the door: Hoyos, Hotel Ton-Po. Yesterday I was talking,
singing, laughing. I'm a normal man, sirs, completely normal. I
prepared chicken with the help of my friend Cárdenas and then I
left. I prefer rice *chaufa*. Better than duck and rice? . . . Go tell
it to your mother! Where have you been wallowing around? I will
speak to your teacher about this. They could have gouged out an
eye. Please, chief, I must ask you again, don't smoke, don't blow
smoke at me. When everything becomes clouded, I'm afraid to see
her that way, as she was, or rather, as she remained. Son, go and
see what is burning. There's a lot of smoke in the kitchen. No,
chief, don't blow smoke in my face. Don't smoke. It causes ghosts
to appear, chief, ghosts. Look, just look there how that Chinaman

with the pipe is watching me, impassively, while I adorn the throat of the doll, the prostitute—Lulu?, Paula?, Gertrudis?—with a bloody smile that stretches from ear to ear.[11]

The references to people, places, and time are purposely made vague. Free association reigns. The smell of cigarette smoke stirs and, in a split second, brings together a confused jumble of memories which span a period of years: "I used to stun butterflies that way. They would fold their wings and go to sleep. Here he is now with the incense! And I, quite the little altar boy, trying not to step on my cassock." Likewise, the memory of a recent act—the preparation of chicken—sparks a sudden recollection of childhood that even contains the speeches of other people: "Go tell it to your mother! Where have you been wallowing around? I will speak to your teacher about this. They could have gouged out an eye." In spite of the studied incoherence of the truncated thoughts and the confused associations, the alert reader has been given sufficient clues in the total context of the story not only to appreciate his intrusion into the character's consciousness but to supply for himself the essential background material for understanding the action.

Of all these writers, Carlos Zavaleta is the most skillful and resourceful in his use of interior monologue. Two stories in particular, "El peregrino" and "Una figurilla," contain excellent examples of indirect interior monologue. Both narratives are similarly structured on two planes of reality: the external world of the present and the protagonists' mental worlds which have no temporal boundaries. The moments in which both protagonist and reader become aware of present, exterior reality serve mainly to provide new stimuli to plunge us back into the stream of consciousness. "Una figurilla," from *La batalla*, in which the present, external world is a small town at night and the mental world is that of a small boy who is somewhat frightened by the prospect of walking alone through dark streets, provides some interesting examples. In both of the following quotations, the lad's observations of his physical surroundings flow quickly and without transition into a reverie about a problem he had at school sometime in the past:

There was nobody in the street. He crossed over to the flagstone sidewalk on the opposite side. No, nobody was around. In school, at least, he didn't feel any loneliness—not even on the last day of examinations when the students in his grade waited fearfully and silently for their turn to appear before a board of five professors. From time to time, a voice from upstairs called out a name, and another student would climb the stairway, passing on the way one who had just been examined. He himself had counted six or seven classmates behind him, each one seated at his desk and dressed up in his best clothes. He had swung his legs back and forth, repeatedly straightened his tie (lent to him by his father), and arranged the folds of his pretty socks so they were just at the right position below his calves. But just when he had begun to feel happy, he had been hit in the back of the neck by a spit ball. Who else could have done it but Marcos? (p. 68)

Nobody was in the street. And there was no moon as he approached the church with its gigantic walls which formed a tower and extended out into a stable where cattle were still gathered during the yearly festivals. There would always be bullfights on the fifth of August. They would fight bulls, oh yes, but (the memory returned) without saying anything to Marcos, he thought about running away someplace where he could again enjoy peace and quiet. But the voice and the claws had been raised again: "Hey, I'm talking to you," howled Marcos, and he kicked the seat of the desk. (p. 69)

The difference between these examples of interior monologue and that employed by Ratto in "Humo" is immediately apparent. Whereas Ratto gives a direct first-person view of his character's consciousness, Zavaleta intervenes to present the mental flow of his character in the third person. In spite of the difference in methods, the purpose of both writers is identical: to communicate the character's psychic life. Zavaleta's method is more controlled, easier to follow, but in both cases there is the same principle of free association, the same absence of temporal limitations, and as a result, the same sense of incoherence.

The real test of the success of such a technique, as Robert Humphrey has indicated in his excellent study of stream-of-consciousness fiction, is whether the writer has been able to "represent the actual texture of consciousness" and "distill some meaning from it to the reader."[12] Ratto has accomplished both ends in "Humo"; Zavaleta has been consistently successful whenever he has used the technique. The other young writers have not always done so well in their attempts to communicate the psychic life of their characters; however, their willingness to experiment with devices for doing so adds an interesting dimension to current Peruvian fiction.

Enrique Congrains Martín's unusual handling of the narrator's point of view in two stories from his collection *Lima, hora cero* is also worth mentioning briefly. Expository passages in the first-person plural alternate with dramatic scenes in the title story which is about the miseries of a group of *gente de barriada*. This technique, in which the point of view is maintained consistently, gives the story a dramatic quality:

Rolling along steadily, we have reached Esperanza. Counting men, women, and children, there are three hundred of us, and we come from all corners of Peru. There are a million of "the others." A million human beings who live within some one hundred and twenty square kilometers. "They" have large gray buildings, splendid houses surrounded by splendid gardens, and luxurious stores which are stocked with everything. (p. 9)

Mateo Torres has arrived here at Esperanza, a "clandestine urban community." Before Mateo there were one hundred of us; when he came, there were one hundred and one, and as the months and years pass our number will reach over three hundred. (p. 14)

The great city grows and grows; it will continue to grow and nobody will be able to stop it. We are located right on its very edge. (p. 16)

Like any other group, we also have our own special laws which fix and establish our way of life in Esperanza. They aren't written down, but we all know them. (p. 17)

It is important to note that these are not the speeches of a narrator-witness in the conventional sense. More accurately they are the words of the collective voice of the *barriada,* a voice that speaks with omniscience. Besides providing an unusual angle of vision with this technique, Congrains succeeds in personalizing the community as a whole, making the reader more sensitive to the existence of many slum dwellers whose words are not heard and whose names are not mentioned.

Equally impressive is "Cuatro pisos, mil esperanzas," a story in which Congrains is able, at times, to establish a striking relationship between point of view, setting, and theme. Much of the narrative consists simply of a conventional rendition by an omniscient author, but there are several unusual scenes in which Congrains experiments successfully with a multiple-view technique. The setting, an apartment complex, lends itself perfectly to this technique, the function of which is to focus on multiple scenes that are occurring simultaneously but in separate locations:

Block four, stairway c, first floor:
"When the *cholo* kids realized that Antonio was sneaking away with the ball, they yelled at him and began to chase him. What a whiz that nigger kid was at running! He caught up to him in the middle of the field, and I couldn't see what happened because . . ."
Block five, stairway b, second floor:
"As soon as the *cholo* kids saw that Antonio was taken care of, they came after us . . ."
"But didn't you say that there were more of you?"
"Yes . . . but they, I don't know, just the sight of them scared us. We knew what we were in for, and in a flash, we started to run."
"Here?"
"No, we couldn't. Since they were spread out on this side, and we

were all bunched up toward the Lima side, they had us cut
off . . ."
"Did you run in that direction?"
"Sure we did, but they began to throw rocks at us, and one hit me
on the head. They surrounded us near the road and began to kick
and punch us . . ."
Block two, stairway b, third floor:
"They were beating the tar out of us when a patrol car passed by.
And then those *cholo* kids began to hit us harder than ever . . ."
(pp. 139–140)

The conversations between the parents and children of the
different apartments happen to concern the loss of a soccer
ball, but that incident in itself adds nothing to the narrative.
What is important is the multiple point of view that allows us
to witness, with a sense of simultaneity, family dramas in
several dwellings and thus experience in a special way the
activity and life in an apartment building. The multiple
viewpoint also serves to underscore the theme: the essential
emptiness and anonymity of the apartment dwellers' lives.
This smallness and lack of vision is captured with great irony
in the everlasting sameness and meaninglessness of their conversations which are repeated time and again with minor
variations from dwelling to dwelling.

This leads us finally to a third, closely related, technical
problem that the writers of the fifties handle with considerable
originality: order, or the temporal structuring of events within
the narrative. In previous periods these events were arranged
in a normal chronological fashion with occasional exceptions
when the author made interesting use of flashback. With the
increased concern to portray the character's consciousness,
however, the problem of order becomes entirely different.
Because of the very nature of the psyche, there is little need,
indeed little appropriateness, in adhering to a rigid chronological order. Within seconds, the mind can flash over a variety
of subjects that are widely separated in time and space. The
psychic life of Zavaleta's two heroes in "El peregrino" and

"Una figurilla," for example, is measured in terms of years. Particularly in the first story, we cover vast chunks of time and space as we follow the rapid, chaotic movement of a young man's mind which ranges, under the principle of free association from the present situation to childhood experiences, to schoolboy activities, back to childhood, etc. The problem, of course, in this abrupt and chaotic breaking of normal chronology is to preserve the necessary clarity and harmony demanded by the art of fiction. Even though the consciousness is fluid, elastic, and disordered, the narrative itself must not lack a design. Using Zavaleta's two stories again as examples, we see that he has carefully framed the stream of consciousness within an external reality. Thus, while the action of the mind covers much time and space, the exterior action lasts only a few minutes and covers but a limited area. In "El peregrino" the exterior action is limited to a short walk to the university. The young hero of "Una figurilla" is in reality never more than a little distance from home and his external activities are of brief duration. In this way, Zavaleta is able to preserve both verisimilitude and order. The temporal structuring of events within a narrative becomes then a more complex technical consideration for the short story writers of the fifties and sixties.

In summary, we have seen that a variety of factors contribute to the current state of the short story in Peru. The emergence of a number of talented young writers since 1950 has resulted in an increase in the volume and vitality of short narrative production. Furthermore, the Peruvian short story has been saved from what had become a restrictive characteristic by the willingness of these men to deal with other than conventional rural settings and characters. Finally, an increased openness to foreign influences and a desire to experiment extensively with new literary techniques have also been positive factors which have added new significance to the short story in Peru.

# ORIGINAL SPANISH PASSAGES

7 Mi estimado amigo: Acabo de leer los *Cuentos malévolos,* que ha tenido a bien darme a conocer antes de entregarlos al público. Me ha movido a leerlos pronto y con interés el saberle a usted joven y el prestigio que para conmigo le presta el nombre de su padre, mi señor don Ricardo, de cuyo ingenio nos queda tan deleitoso dejo a todos los que le hemos leído. Quería ver si corroboraba aquel decidero: *de tal palo tal astilla,* y todos los de la misma suerte, que no son pocos. Y le aseguro que no se han quebrado mis esperanzas.

10 El buen Ernesto no creía en el mal; decía que los hombres y las mujeres eran inmejorables, y que la maldad se revelaba en ellos como una forma pasajera, como una condición fugaz, como una crisis efímera . . . como una ráfaga que pasaba por el alma humana sin dejar huellas; la maldad era, según él, un estado anormal como la borrachera o la enfermedad.

11 Nazareno, has sido un sublime visionario, creíste redimirnos y no nos has redimido. S.M. el Pecado reina hoy tan omnipotente como antes y más que antes. El pecado original, de cuya mancha quisiste lavarnos es nuestro más deleitoso y adorado pecado.

11 Tú querías salvar a la Humanidad y no la salvarás; porque la salvación que tú ofreces es la muerte y la Humanidad quiere vivir, y la vida es mi aliento. . . . Sabe, ¡oh desventurado mártir! que yo soy la Carne, que yo soy el Deseo, que yo soy la Ciencia, que yo soy la Pasión, que yo

163

soy la Curiosidad, que yo soy todas las energías y estímulos de la naturaleza viva, que yo soy todo lo que invita al hombre a vivir.

12   Por todas partes se veían las enmarañadas copas de árboles extraños, cuyos troncos estaban llenos de pústulas. El aire tenía un olor repugnante, como el de la sala de un hospital de gangrenados. Las aves, que cruzaban el espacio, tenían los curepos purulentos, con una que otra pluma desmalazada: volaban tardamente, lanzando graznidos lastimeros; las fieras cruzaban nuestro camino con paso dificultoso de bestias baldadas por la elefantíasis, tiñosa la piel y los ijares hundidos, como interiormente corroídos por un mal implacable. Las flores, apenas abiertas, caían moribundas sobre el césped raquítico y gris; sus pétalos ardían en violenta fiebre, y sus estambres se estremecían y retorcían en las convulsiones de intenso dolor. . . . Una leona con su cría reposaba echada en medio del camino; estaba desfallecida y con el cuerpo cubierto de pústulas sobre las que saltaban moscas verdes. . . . La pobre bestia yacía con la lengua fuera, jadeante y quejumbrosa, mientras sus cachorros, flacos como galgos, con la desvencijada columna dorsal rompiéndoles la piel, se afanaban por mamar de unas ubres vacías y lacias de las que no manaba sino sangre viciada.

14   significa una novedad, una impulsión rara que mortifique el pensamiento y sacuda violentamente nuestra ya gastado mecanismo nervioso.

15   Su entrada produjo una verdadera revolución. Millones de cucarachas rojas se pusieron en movimiento. . . . Había sitios en los que el muro se había derrumbado y formado pequeños montes de barro y piedras, y sobre los que tenía que pasar Feliciano; allí tenían los sapos su madriguera; allí también había culebras . . . y lombrices, que al ser pisadas por Feliciano se enroscaban a sus pies en los estertores de la agonía.

15   En otra calle . . . vió un animalejo del tamaño de un puño; dirigió la linterna hacia él: era una enorme araña en cuyo vientre podía caber un colibrí. La araña le miraba con sus ocho ojillos fulgurantes y emponzoñados, como las puntas de ocho flechas empapadas de curare. Estaban erizados sus pelos, y sobre el coselete se veía la palpitación ansiosa de un luchador que esperaba la agresión. . . . En otro lugar

encontró un matrimonio de escuerzos; la enorme bocaza de
los dos animales parecía contraída por una sempiterna
sonrisa, en tanto que las miradas de sus ojos parecían
perderse en ensueños de una voluptuosidad estúpida. . . .
De un puntapié les arrojó . . . al agua y allí se sumergieron
alegremente para posar después sus amores sobre otra
piedra.

15  Nos creímos acaso andrógenos y cruzábamos los misterios de
la noche vinculados por una entrañable fraternidad asex-
uada.

16  tenía la delicada pureza de una virginidad cristalizada,
el encanto infantil y la gracia de una adolescencia detenida.

16  Nuestros locuras y caprichos debían matarla y así fue. Su
cuerpo . . . había nacido para el amor burgués, metódico,
sereno, higiénico, y no para el amor loco, inquieto y
extenuante exigido por nuestros cerebros llenos de curiosi-
dades malsanas, por nuestras fantasías bullentes y atrevidas,
por nuestros nervios siempre anhelantes de sensaciones
fuertes y nuevas.

18  Cierto que Vassielich, un buen hombre que jamás me había
hecho daño alguno, iba a sufrir mucho con esta desgracia,
pero ¿a mí qué me importaba?, ¿perdía yo algo con el
desastre de Vassielich? No, al contrario, ganaba una div-
ersión durante el trayecto del puente, que tiene unos cien
metros de largo.

19  Tras de rápida y tranquila selección de los géneros de
muerte al uso en los suicidios, elegí la horca. Tenía noticias
de que los ahorcados tienen una muerte dulce y se me había
asegurado que, en los pocos segundos en que el sujeto físico
se debate en las convulsiones agónicas, se produce una
delectable sensación.

20  Créame que siento sincero afecto por usted que tanto me ha
prodigado su desinteresado interés para que aplace el acto
de danza aérea con que me propongo poner fin a mi
descolorida historia. Y siento también mucha pena de
rehusar por mi parte la vieja oferta que hizo usted a nuestros
progenitores en el Edén; me refiero al atracón de frutos del
árbol de la Ciencia del Bien y del Mal, del que sufrieron
serias indigestiones no sólo nuestros primeros padres, sino
Raimundo Lulio y la cáfila de alquimistas de la edad media.
¿Para qué resumir o mejor dicho abarcar en un solo conjunto

todo lo cognoscible y lo incognoscible, cuando, sin apuro, pacientemente, gradualmente, estamos dejando agotado el arbolito paradisiaco? . . . Pues se irá mordiendo poco a poco en el curso de los siglos y descorriéndose todos los velos, y conociéndose todas las verdades hasta llegar a la última verdad, que no sería extraño fuera la de que todo es una mentira.

20 floraciones de mi escepticismo desconcertante . . . cuentos inspirados en los bajos fondos del espíritu humano . . . cuentos de pasiones complicadas y anormales, cuentos de fantasía descarriada de ironía amarga y resignada.

27 Yo el sexto de mis hermanos, nací algunos años después de la guerra. Mi padre no tenía trabajo, y para buscarlo se había alejado a otros pueblos. Tendría yo seis años, y el mayor de mis hermanos dieciocho. . . . Yo recuerdo con espanto y con ternura aquellos días de mi infancia. Imaginad a mi madre rodeada de seis niños despertando a la vida y dándose cuenta de tan terrible drama. Formábamos unidos un grupo contra el destino, y como para defendernos de él, nos abrazábamos más estrechamente. Más tarde jamás nos hemos separado y creo que esta solidaridad que nos ha unido toda la vida, no es sino la continuación de aquel sentimiento que nos hizo comprender entonces, la necesidad de ampararnos unos a otros, mientras mi madre pálida, insomne, desgarrada, lloraba en silencio por ella, por nosotros, por nuestro porvenir, por nuestra niñez infortunada y sin risas.

31 Junto al bote, duerme el hombre del mar, el fuerte mancebo, embriagado por la brisa caliente y por la tibia emanación de la arena . . . el fuerte pecho desnudo . . . se levanta rítmicamente, con el ritmo de la Vida, el más armonioso que Dios ha puesto sobre el mundo.

31 Jamás riña alguna manchó sus claros anales; morales y austeros, labios de marido besaron siempre labios de esposa; y el amor, fuente inagotable de odios y maldecires, era, entre ellos, tan normal y apacible como el agua de sus pozos.

31 En el fondo del desierto, como si temieran su silenciosa aridez, las palmeras únense en pequeños grupos, tal como lo hacen los peregrinos al cruzarlo y, ante el peligro, los hombres.

31 Era el eterno enemigo de la gente . . . de los pescadores que se lanzaban en los frágiles botes, de las mujeres que los

esperaban temerosas, a la caída de la tarde; el eterno enemigo de todos que viven a la orilla. El terrible enemigo . . . que a veces es el remolino desconocido y siniestro que lleva a los pescadores hacia el vórtice extraño y no los deja volver más a la costa.

32 Amanecía en Pisco, alegremente . . . en el radiante despertar del día, sentíamos los pasos de mi madre en el comedor, preparando el café para papá . . . oíase el canto del gallo que era contestado a intervalos por todos los de la vecindad . . . sentíase el ruido del mar, el frescor de la mañana. Después mi madre venía a nosotros, nos hacía rezar, arrodillados en la cama con nuestras blancas camisas de dormir.

32 La comida fue en silencio. Mamá no tomó nada. Y en el mutismo de esa noche triste yo veía que mamá no quitaba la vista del lugar que debía ocupar mi padre . . . sólo se oía el chocar de los cubiertos con los platos o los pasos apagados de la sirvienta, o el rumor que producía el viento al doblar los árboles del jardín. Mamá sólo dijo dos veces con su voz dulce y triste:

—Niño, no se toma así la cuchara.

—Niña, no se come tan de prisa.

33 A la orilla del mar se piensa siempre; hay el continuo ir y venir de las olas; la perenne visión del horizonte; los barcos que cruzan el mar a lo lejos sin que nadie sepa su origen o rumbo; las neblinas matinales durante las cuales los buques perdidos pitean clamorosamente, como buscándose unos a otros en la bruma cual ánimas desconsoladas en el mundo de las sombras.

33 En mi casa, mi dormitorio tenía una ventana que daba hacia el jardín cuya única vid desmedrada y raquítica, de hojas carcomidas por el salitre serpenteaba agarrándose en los barrotes oxidados. Al despertar abría yo los ojos y contemplaba, tras el jardín, el mar. Por allí cruzaban los vapores con su plomiza cabellera de humo que se diluía en el cielo azul. Otros llegaban al puerto, creciendo poco a poco, rodeados de gaviotas que flotaban a su lado como copos de espuma y, ya fondeados, los rodeaban pequeños botecillos ágiles. Eran entonces los barcos como cadáveres de insectos, acosados por hormigas hambrientas.

34 Anduve largo rato y pronto me encontré en la mitad del camino. Al norte, el puerto ya lejano de Pisco aparecía

envuelto en un vapor vibrante, veíanse las casas muy pequeñas y los pinos, casi borrados por la distancia. . . . Los barcos del puerto tenían un aspecto de abandono, cual si estuvieran varados por el viento del sur. . . . Ante la soledad del paisaje, sentí cierto temor que me detuvo. . . . En medio de esa hora me sentí solo, aislado, y tuve la idea de haberme perdido en una de esas playas desconocidas y remotas, blancas y solitarias a donde van las aves a morir. Entonces sentí el divino prodigio del silencio; poco a poco se fue callando el rumor de las olas, yo estaba inmóvil en la curva de la playa. . . . Nada acusaba ya a la humanidad ni a la vida. Todo era mudo y muerto.

35  El otro, que en verdad no parecía ser un gallo fino de distinguida sangre y alcurnia hacía cosas tan petulantes cuan humanas.

36  Papá nos hizo salir, cruzamos las calles, tomamos el cochecito y yo, mudo y triste, oyendo los comentarios, no sé qué cosas pensaba contra esa gente. Por primera vez comprendí que había hombres muy malos.

38  Yo quisiera representar en un pequeño trozo lo que ven mis ojos. Aprisionar la naturaleza. Hacer lo que hace el río con los árboles y con el cielo. Reproducirlos. Pero me faltan colores, los colores no me dan la idea de lo que yo tengo en el alma.

38  Ella me dijo: ¡Chasca, Chasca! ¡Amame más, ámame más, ámame una vez aún! ¡Aunque después arrojes mi cuerpo al río o me dejes en la roca para que los cóndores se ceben, aunque cojas mis cabellos para tus trofeos, y mi piel para tus tambores y mis dientes para tus amuletos, ámame, ámame una vez más, ámame más! . . . Y se colgó a mi cuello y sonidos inarticulados y roncos salían de su garganta fuerte y sus labios quemaban y estaban secos y sus ojos ardían con una extraña llama.

40  Mi abuela parecía al principio reparar poco en mí. Se diría que mi presencia le causaba algún arrepentimiento. Y posiblemente era así. Para una mujer tan católica, que solía confesarse por la Cuaresma, yo no podía menos que significarle la falta del hijo. . . . Cuanto a mi tía Isabel, parecía no haberme advertido. Me miraba de reojo, no me dirigía la palabra sino por parábola, es decir, pasando por encima del parentesco, haciendo distinciones odiosas que mi

precocidad recogía al vuelo y vaciaba en el acervo de mis pequeñas tristezas, haciéndome llorar a hurtadillas en algún rincón perdido de la casona.

40 Esta vida de casa grande, de constante e imprescindible movimiento, en la que todo parecía moverse por cuenta propia y, al parecer, sin relación alguna, fue acostumbrándome a la iniciativa y a la acción, al dominio de mí mismo y a sacar del abandono y del desvío, fuerzas de agresividad y de triunfo. Aprendí a tener la boca pronta para la réplica hiriente, a recibir y devolver las frases soslayadas, a corresponder con los puños o con cualquier cosa los golpes que recibía de los primos, a mirar de frente y con soberbia a las gentes que me miraban con sorna; en una palabra, a confiar sólo en mí.

46 "Te llevas toda mi cosecha, taita. Por eso me decía Niceta: Oye, Marcelo, ¿no te parece bueno que Benito estudie también para cura? ¿Para qué?, le respondí yo. Y ella me contestó . . . Para que trabaje menos y gane más, como taita Ramun."

48 —Viejo, aquí te traigo a tu hija para que no la hagas buscar tanto. . . . Y, sin esperar respuesta, el hombre, que no era otro que Hilario Crispín, desató el saco y vació de golpe el contenido, un contenido nauseabundo. . . . Aquello era la hija de Tucto. . . . Pero el viejo . . . exclamó:
—Harás bien en llevarte tu saco; será robado y me traería mala suerte. Pero ya que me has traído a mi hija debes dejar algo para las velas del velorio y para atender a los que vengan a acompañarme. ¿No tendrás siquiera un sol?

57 Y fue en aquel momento cuando el niño bisoño se echó a llorar de rabia y de vergüenza también. ¿Era él, él mismo, quien había cometido aquel robo patente, aquel abuso de fuerza? ¿De qué abuelo conquistador le había venido de pronto la torva brutalidad?

57 Y entonces sacó de entre sus bártulos el pequeño *Código de Napoleón,* y arrimándose al borde del camino, lo largó al barranco de los cóndores con todo un paquete de ideas civilizadas y de ilusiones inútiles.

58 Los brujos de la tribu *sensi* sepan más cosas incógnitas de la tierra y del cielo que estos diablos extranjeros que usan barbas de mono y se visten de *pampanillas* como las hembras.

59   es decir, ha aprendido a mentir, que roba los maridos a las
     demás mujeres y que se niega a bañarse de la mañana a la
     noche, como sus compañeras, en los sagrados ríos de mi
     tierra.

59   ¡Espléndida criatura, nacida del sueño de una noche de
     verano! Si los etnógrafos no nos jurasen que esta raza
     procede de las altiplanicies del Asia o de las islas del
     Pacífico, creeríamos no pocas veces que ha salido de los
     cuadros del Renacimiento o de los primitivos italianos. Esos
     ojos aterciopelados de ternura, la tez dorada por el rever-
     berar de las nieves.

59   El admirable pecho de la chiquilla se abultaba bajo un
     extraño manto. . . . Y los delicados pies, llenos de polvo en
     las sandalias burdas, tenían una gracia bíblica.

59   ¿Quién iba a quererme así, pisando las huellas de mi caballo,
     en busca del Amado por los caminos, como en el excelso
     cantar de Salamón? ¿Cuál otra me perseguiría también,
     desmelenada, olvidando a los suyos y entregándose para
     toda la vida?

72   El carácter de la propiedad agraria en el Perú constituye uno
     de los peores obstáculos al desarrollo del capitalismo na-
     cional. El obstáculo radica principalmente en la equivocada
     noción económica del latifundista de interesarse únicamente
     en la rentabilidad de sus tierras y no en su productividad.
     Empeoran la situación el sistema del propietario ausente y la
     falta de crédito al pequeño arrendatario.

73   Las haciendas de la costa peruana no atienden la salubridad
     de sus braceros, de allí que el paludismo arrase la población
     rural costeña compuesta principalmente de cholos e indios.

83   En la forma más sencilla, don Evaristo Claro comentó
     sonriendo:
     —A las minas La Poderosa ha llegado un ingeniero de Lima.
     Mozo, muy mozo todavía. De unos treinta años. Parece que
     en los dos meses que lleva ahí ha compuesto ese berengenal
     de los demonios.
     —Ajá.
     —Y me han dicho, yo no lo sé, que todos los viernes, por las
     noches, baja a Pacarán en lugar de quedarse en el campa-
     mento; yo cuento y no comento.
     Merino sonrió a su vez:
     —Será porque tiene frío. Usted sabe que esa puna. Y estos

mocositos limeños, apenas les falta la cobija de la madre se echan a llorar, ¿no es cierto?

—Algunos. Otros, no. Y a éste, no le conocemos la pinta.

Se encrespó con la alusión el notario:

—¿Qué me quiere usted decir, mi señor don Evaristo?

—¡Hombre! ¿Yo? nada.

84 Yo pienso y siento en zambo. Se me perdió el anillo de armas en una jarana del Callao, porque tuve que empeñarlo para tentar, con pisco, a una prieta zamarra que retozaba en el vuelo de un tondero. Y allá me quedé, aún cuando esté en París, en ese galpón de mulatas, en el solar preclaro de los criollos, abrazado a la vihuela para enamorar chinitas.

85 Pensé, como pienso ahora, que un "Literato," en la noble acepción del vocablo, debe ser, absolutamente, un agnóstico en política. Puede y debe un escritor reflejar el ambiente y el medio social y ser, por ende, un escritor social, mas creo que no debe un escritor limitar su arte dentro de una consigna de partido. . . . La vida no tiene partido político alguno y el amor, el odio, los celos, la aventura, el hijo, el padre, son idénticos en el Soviet, en el Fascio y en el Nazismo. Por esto me parece absurdo pretender reflejar, artísticamente, las preocupaciones políticas porque, además, eso se hace más eficazmente en forma directa en un libro, absolutamente político, un discurso, un manifiesto: en un poema o una novela, jamás.

89 Se va a notar que un sentimiento de dolor corre por las páginas de mi libro. Esto parecerá extraño a quien conozca la selva americana sólo de referencia. Es decir, al que no la haya vivido. Pero quien cruzó sus senderos o navegó sus ríos, sabrá intuir por qué estos cuentos no son alegres. La selva es triste y todo contribuye a que así sea . . .

90 Dentro de ella nos sentimos moral y físicamente pequeños. Tristes. Y sobresaltados. Porque todo nos acecha. Las hojas secas que pisamos, el árbol que nos cubre del sol, el tronco en que nos recostamos, el agua que bebemos, el fruto que se nos ofrece. Cada una de estas sencillas formas vitales que aisladamente nos protegerían, unidas en el bosque están prestas a atacarnos, a destruirnos. La víbora brota aleve, las hojas emanan efluvios nocivos, los troncos albergan insectos dañinos, el agua guarda gérmenes enfermizos, el fruto nos entrega veneno, los animales atacan. Nosotros mismos nos

angustiamos. La imaginación excitada hace que nuestros ojos vean seres sobrenaturales que nos hostilizan y nos burlan. Son los demonios del bosque. Innumerables. Crueles.

Si hasta las creaciones de nuestra inteligencia nos acechan, ¿dónde encontrar alegría en la selva?

91   He aquí ocho cuentos que sólo quiero que reciban la calificación de peruanos. A esta inmensidad geográfica que es lo nuestro—inmensidad partida en trozos—entrégolos, como los primeros que publicara, imponiéndoles la misión de que contribuyan a que el Perú se conozca a sí mismo.

95   —La Yunsa. ¡La Yunsa!—gritaron otros.—Vamo a comenzar.

—Ay va—contestaron los músicos. Y la canción rompió vibrante:

> "Yunsita, yunsita
> ¿Quién te tumbará?
> Já já."

Salieron los danzantes y comenzó el baile en ronda:

> "Y el que tumbare
> te renovará
> Já já."

Se separó una pareja. El hombre armado de hacha cuyos golpes herían el tronco, silencioso pero quizá dolorido. Cambiaron de letra:

> "Saucesito verde
> color de la playa.
> Priéstame tu sombra
> hasta que me vaya."

La mujer tomaba el hacha y golpeaba a su vez.

Así siguió la fiesta y ya la Yunsa se iba debilitando. Con un quejido se inclinaba suavemente a un lado. Los peones se alegraban cada vez más y el pisco daba vueltas más frecuentes, avivando rescoldos de pasión.

108   Después de saludarlo paso a decirle . . . ¡Por los clavos! Críe usted cuervos para que le saquen los ojos. Otra ronda, don Rafo. De lo mismo, por variar . . . Mis hijos, Paucha. Cierra el hocico, "Tamalazo." Tus hijos son unos pelmas. ¿Vas a comparar a alguno de ellos con Juanito? Muchacho para inteligente . . . todos los premios de la escuela se sacó este año. ¿No lo sabes?

Espectativas . . . Mi porvenir . . . ¿Pero qué se había imaginado el muy ingrato? ¿Acaso Santos Paucha no pensaba en todo? ¿Quién sino él lo iba a sustituir en la guardianía? Mi porvenir . . . Cimarrón, desamorado. ¿Qué decirle ahora a la Asunta? Don Rafo: destápese usted un par de botellas del tinto especial. Del especial, ¡ah!

¿Y la vigilancia de la zona norte? Iba a tener que limpiar solo las piedras de Caleta Pelada. . . . Guárdame la carabinita que me regalaste . . . ¿Para qué? Las armas no son para maricones que se escapan. . . . Verdad don Rafo. Verdad. Más copas, "Tamalazo." Conque tus hijos . . . ¡Ah! Juan es hombre para cada uno de ellos y hasta para todos juntos. Ingrato. Largarse ahora, en la época de anidación, cuando más lo necesito. Porque las primeras parejas de guanayes y piqueros están ya formando nido en los barrancos, Juan. Ayer llegaron. Mi porvenir . . . Yo no puedo vivir en la guardianía. ¿Qué quiere, el desgraciado?

120 —Está bien que ante las imágenes y cruces pongan lámparas y velas . . . ¡pero piedras!

—Como que da lo mesmo, patroncito. La piedra es también devoción. El indio se quedó meditando y luego, esforzándose por dar expresión adecuada a sus pensamientos, dijo lentamente:—Mire patroncito. La piedra no es cosa de depreciarla. ¿Qué fuera del mundo sin la piedra? Se hundiría. La piedra sostiene la tierra. Como que sostiene la vida.

122 Dentro del problema, el mestizo desempeña un papel de enlace entre la tradición y la vida nueva. Guardando en sí valores antiguos y estando en circunstancias sociales más propicias para adquirir los elementos educacionales y econó micos de la liberación, trae a la vida americana un tácito o explícito acento reivindicador.

124 Perdóneme, don Pedro . . . Claro que ésta no es manera de presentarme . . . Pero, le diré . . . ¿Cómo podría explicarle? . . . Ha muerto Eusebio López . . . Ya sé que usted no lo conoce y muy pocos lo conocían . . . ¿Quién se va a fijar en un hombre que vive entre tablas viejas? . . . Por eso no fui a traer los ladrillos . . . Eramos amigos, ¿me entiende?

125 ¡Ese olor! Usted comprende, don Pedro . . . Lo olíamos allá, en el Pacífico . . . Es el olor de los muertos, los japoneses . . . Los muertos son lo mismo . . . Sólo que como nosotros, allá, íbamos avanzando . . . a nuestros her-

idos y muertos, los recogían y encontrábamos muertos
japoneses de días, pudriéndose . . . Ahora Cheo López
comenzaba a oler así . . .

126    solían salir al espacio talado y estiraban los brazos ante la luz,
con un aire de aves fatigadas.

126    Era un sesentón membrudo de ojos de jaguar y la consabida
barba enmarañada y sucia. La piel blanca había adquirido
tonos ocres y verdosos tal si se le hubieran pegado del
bosque, y las barbazas grises parecían un manojo de esos
bejucos parásitos que cuelgan de los troncos.

129    Escribí el primer relato en el castellano más correcto y
"literario" que podía alcanzar. Leí después el cuento a
algunos de mis amigos de Lima, y lo elogiaron. Pero yo
detestaba cada vez más aquellas páginas. ¡No, no eran así ni
el hombre, ni el pueblo, ni el paisaje que yo quería
describir, casi podía decir, denunciar! Bajo un falso lenguaje
se mostraba un mundo como inventado, sin médula y sin
sangre; un típico mundo "literario," en que la palabra ha
consumido a la obra. Mientras en la memoria, en mi interior,
el verdadero tema seguía ardiendo, intocado. Volví a escribir
el relato, y comprendí definitivamente que el castellano no
me serviría si seguía empleándolo en la forma tradicional-
mente literaria.

133    Llegué al pie del molino, subí a la pared más alta y miré
desde allí la cabeza del "Chawala": el cerro medio negro,
recto, amenazaba caerse sobre los alfalfares de la hacienda.
Daba miedo por las noches; los indios nunca lo miraban a
esas horas y en las noches claras conversaban siempre dando
espaldas al cerro.

133    El Ak'chi es nada en Ak'ola. . . . En vano . . . se molesta,
en vano tiene aire de tayta, de "Señor," nada hace en esas
tierras; para el paradero de las nubes nomás sirve.

133    Mariano había crecido bajo la protección de un río pequeño.

133    La noche del 23 de junio esos arpistas descendían por el
cauce de los riachuelos que caen en torrentes al río
profundo, al río principal que lleva su caudal a la costa. Allí,
bajo las grandes cataratas que sobre roca negra forman los
torrentes, los arpistas "oían." ¡Sólo esa noche el agua crea
melodías nuevas al caer sobre la roca y rodando en su
lustroso cauce! Cada maestro arpista tiene su pak'cha (salto

de agua) secreta. Se echa, de pecho, escondido bajo los penachos . . . algunos se cuelgan de los troncos . . . sobre el abismo en que el torrente se precipita y llora. Al día siguiente, y durante todas las fiestas del año, cada arpista toca melodías nunca oídas. Directamente al corazón, el río les dicta música nueva.

134   El tayta Inti quería, seguro, la muerte de la tierra, miraba de frente, de todas sus fuerzas. Su rabia hacía arder al mundo y hacía llorar a los hombres.

134   El sol brillaba con fuerza en el cielo limpio; su luz blanca me calentaba el cuerpo con cariño, se tendía sobre la quebrada, y sobre los cerros lejanos. . . . Los cernícalos peleaban alegres en el aire; los pichiuchas gritoneaban sobre los montoncitos de taya y sunchu. Todo el mundo parecía contento. En la cabecera de Ak'ola, el agua de Jatunkocha, de la cual tomaba el pueblo, se arrojaba cantando sobre la roca negra.

135   El chaucato ve a la víbora y la denuncia; su lírica voz se descompone. Cuando descubre a la serpiente venenosa lanza un silbido, más de alarma que de espanto, y otros chaucatos vuelan agitadamente hacia el sitio del descubrimiento; se posan cerca, miran el suelo con simulado espanto y llaman, saltando, alborotando. Los campesinos acuden con urgencia, buscan el reptil y lo parten a machetazos.

135   Nunca se funden las cosas del mundo como en esa luz. El resplandor de las estrellas llega hasta el fondo, a la materia de las cosas, a los montes y ríos, al color de los animales y flores, al corazón humano, cristalinamente; y todo está unido por ese resplandor silencioso. Desaparece la distancia. El hombre galopa pero los astros cantan en su alma, vibran en sus manos. No hay alto cielo.

136   El fresco de la mañana, la alegría de la quebrada madre, me consolaba de nuevo.

136   Confiado y valiente estaba yo esta mañana. . . . La altivez de tayta Ak'chi, la alegría de los potreros y los montes, el volar orgulloso de los gavilanes y los killinchos (cernícalos) me enardecían la sangre; me volví atrevido.

136   Sobre las pampas frías . . . las vicuñitas gritan, mirando tristemente a los viajeros que pasan por el camino. Los indios tienen corazón para este animalito, le quieren; en sus

ojos turbios prende una ternura muy dulce cuando se la quedan mirando, allá, sobre los cerros blancos de la puna, mientras gritan con su voz triste y delgada.

136 en su boca de labios abultados, en sus ojos legañosos y azules, en sus orejas pequeñas, encontrábamos una expresión de bondad que nos desleía el corazon. ¡"Gringacha"! . . . La quería como a una madre de verdad.

136 ¡Mamacha, Gringacha! Me eché sobre el cuello blanco de la Gringa, y lloré. . . . Su cuerpo caliente, su olor a leche fresca, se acababan poco a poco, junto con mi alegría.

137 El cernícalo lo miraba con inteligencia. El rostro del músico se reflejaba resplandeciente de felicidad en los ojos profundos del cernícalo. Mariano tocaba una danza guerrera de carnaval y luego bailaba a grandes saltos, sin dejar de mirar a la pequeña ave de nariz acerada. —¡Son amigos! ¡Se entienden! ¡La misma alma tienen, seguro!—exclamaba Antolín, observando que en esos instantes de regocijo, Mariano y el cernícalo no dejaban de mirarse. El corazón del "Upa" está palpitando como si fuera killincho (cernícalo).

137 "Agua" sí fue escrita con odio, con el arrebato de un odio puro; aquél que brota de los amores universales, allí, en las regiones del mundo donde existen dos bandos enfrentados con primitiva crueldad.

Porque los relatos de "Agua" contienen la vida de una aldea andina de Perú, en que los personajes de las facciones tradicionales se reducen, muestran y enfrentan nítidamente. Allí no viven sino dos clases de gentes que representan dos mundos implacable y esencialmente distintos; el terrateniente convencido hasta la médula, por la acción de los siglos, de su superioridad humana sobre los indios; y los indios, que han conservado con más ahinco la unidad de su cultura, por el mismo hecho de estar sometidos y enfrentados a una tan fanática y bárbara fuerza.

139 Doña Josefa rasgueaba fuerte la guitarra; los concertados y las otras mujeres palmeaban, y le daban ánimo a la pareja. Sin necesidad de aguardiente y sin chicha, doña Josefa sabía alegrarnos, sabía hacernos bailar. Los comuneros no eran disimulados para ella, no eran callados y sonsos como delante del principal; su verdadero corazón le mostraban a ella, su verdadero corazón sencillo y amoroso.

145 Ahora, hermanos, toca descanso. Todo el día tras el escrito-

rio: papeles, memorándums, órdenes, facturas, ¡basta ahora!
La vida es como el color de las paredes y de los edificios:
colores optimistas, pero sólo optimistas. Colores fáciles:
amarillo, anaranjado, verde, azul, crema, guinda suave,
celeste. La persona que planeó estos edificios evitó cuidado-
samente los grises, los marrones, los plomos lúgubres. Mejor
dicho: podemos vivir en una torre de marfil. Aquí no
tenemos ni latas, ni cartones, ni maderas podridas, ni barro,
ni quincha, ni esteras pajizas, ni excrementos alrededor de
uno. Estamos bien, hermanos; nuestros hijos pueden crecer
en su maravillosa torre de marfil; nosotros, contentos,
podemos morir a mitades: mitad aquí, en Matute, mitad
allá, tras los escritorios. ¿Y por qué no? Con estos colores,
con estos tonos, con nuestra quincena, con nuestra comida ni
buena ni mala, con nuestra alegría mediocre, con nuestros
problemas ni infinitos ni desesperantes, con nuestra mujer,
cariñosa y feliz, con nuestro radio y nuestro cinema, con
nuestras fiestas y borracheras de vez en cuando, con nuestros
hijos que algún día nos calcarán, con todo eso que forma
nuestra vida, bien vale la pena que nos consideremos y que
nos engañemos: ¡somos felices! ¡somos hombres!

146 —Mamá, ¿la viejita de las gallinas no tendrá frío de
noche?
—No sé . . . ¿y qué importa si tiene frío, después de
todo?

146 —Mamá, ¿y la viejita de las gallinas no tendrá hambre?
—No sé, hijita . . . y además, ¿qué importa si tiene
hambre, después de todo?

146 —Mamá, ¿y si los hijitos de la viejita no tienen juguetes?
—Mira hijita, no pienses tonterías: esos chicos no conocen lo
que son juguetes. Cualquier cosa les sirve: piedrecitas,
latitas, tablitas, pollitos, no te preocupes, mi hijita, que ellos
tienen sus propios juguetes.

151 los indios y los borrachos se habían espantado de que
Chueca tomara una rienda y zurriara salvajemente al cóndor,
de que se detuviera debajo mismo de la sombra que le
protegía del sol y lo flagelara entre insultos y el alucinado
chisporroteo de la sangre . . . media hora más tarde el
cóndor no había muerto aún: ahí estaban sus garras libres, su
pico rojo, un coágulo o una flor de sangre, y ahí estaba el
charco maldito y crecido, lamido y besado por los perros.

Chueca bebía más chicha y flagelaba más y mejor; y, en un instante, desde su caballo, aferró una pata del animal y se la fue tirando a pocos, enloquecido por la fuerza de los huesos, de los insospechados metales habidos en la carne. Los indios se hicieron a un lado y las guitarras se acallaron, y ahí estuvo Chueca, borracho, cayéndose de la montura, si bien insultando y echando espumarajos. Hasta que colgóse de nuevo de las patas, de las plumas, y hombre y animal se hundieron, rotas las ligaduras. Mas tampoco fue ése el fin. Ahí se levantó el verdugo a hundir sus botas en el pecho, a beber una mar de sangre, hasta errar un puntapié y caerse él también junto al cóndor, que le miraba y le lanzaba su jadeo, sus dignos y débiles graznidos. Ya ni las alas se movieron entonces: apenas si los garfios de las patas se abrían y cerraban por cosa de los golpes. Y seguía el salvaje hablándole borracho a la tierra y a las plumas deshojadas, vejando a la escombra del pájaro aún vivo y golpeando a los indios que buscaban dejarle en dos pies.

156    ¡No me eche el humo en la cara! Así atontaba yo mariposas: plegaban las alas y se dormían. ¡Ahora el del incienso! Y yo muy monaguillo tratando de no pisarme la sotana. Prefiero tocar la campanilla, padre. Acaban de abrir la puerta: Hoyos, hotel Ton-Po. Ayer estuve hablando, cantando, riendo. Soy un hombre normal, señores, completamente normal. Preparé la polla con mi amigo Cárdenas, y me fui. Yo prefiero el arroz chaufa. ¿Al arroz con pato? . . . ¡Eso se lo vas a repetir a tu madre! ¿Dónde te has estado revolcando? Hablaré con tu profesor. Te han podido sacar un ojo. Por favor, jefe, le repito, no fume, no me eche el humo. Que cuando todo se nubla temo verla así, tal como estaba, mejor, así como quedó. Hijo, anda a ver qué se está quemando. Hay mucho humo en la cocina. No, jefe, no me tire el humo, no fume. Que surgen los fantasmas, jefe, los fantasmas. Mire, mire cómo me observa impasible con su pipa el chino aquel, mientras a ella, la muñeca, la mariposa, ¿Lulú, Paula, Gertrudis? le cuelgo en el cuello una sangrienta sonrisa de oreja a oreja.

158    No había nadie en la calle. Cruzó hacia la otra vereda de lajas. No, no había nadie. Soledad, por lo menos, no había en la escuela, y ni siquiera la había habido en el último día de los exámenes, cuando los alumnos de su año aguardaban

temerosos, y en silencio, ser llamados de uno en uno a comparecer ante el jurado de cinco profesores. De tiempo en tiempo, la voz de los altos llamaba un nombre y un nuevo alumno iba a cruzarse, al subir las escaleras, con quien ya había rendido examen. El mismo había contado seis o siete compañeros a sus espaldas, cada cual en su carpeta y vestidos, se diría, para una fiesta. Había columpiado sus piernas, alisado muchas veces la corbata de su padre y el doblez de sus lindas medias abajo de las pantorrillas. Pero entonces, cuando ya se sentía feliz, había recibido en la nuca un proyectil de papel mojado. ¿Quién podía ser, sino Marcos?

158    Y no había nadie en la calle. Y no había luna y allegábase ya a la iglesia, a los gigantes muros que seguían en la armazón de la torre y se alargaban todavía en el establo donde se hacinaban las reses durante las fiestas de cada año. Toreaban, entonces, los días cinco de agosto. Toreaban, oh sí, mas (volvió el recuerdo), sin decir nada a Marcos, pensó en la fuga que le llevaría de nuevo al silencio. Empero, la voz y las zarpas habíanse alzado también: —¡Oy, tistoy hab-blando! —aulló Marcos y lanzó un puntapié a las tablas que formaban el asiento de la carpeta.

159    Rodando, tumbo a tumbo, hemos llegado a Esperanza. Somos más de trescientos entre hombres, mujeres y niños, y provenimos de todos los rincones del Perú. "Los otros" son un millón. Un millón de seres que viven dentro de unos ciento veinte kilómetros cuadrados, aproximadamente. "Ellos" tienen inmensos edificios grises; espléndidas casas, rodeadas de espléndidos jardines; tiendas lujosas provistas de todo.

159    Es aquí, a Esperanza, una "urbanización clandestina", a donde ha llegado Mateo Torres. En ese entonces éramos unos cien, con Mateo fuimos uno más, y con el correr de meses y años llegamos a más de trescientos.

159    La gran ciudad crece, crece y seguirá creciendo sin que nadie la pueda detener. Y nosotros estamos en su mismo borde.

160    Como cualquier colectividad humana, nosotros también tenemos leyes propias y particulares que fijan y establecen normas de vida en Esperanza. No están escritas, pero todos los conocemos.

160    Block cuarto, escalera c, primer piso:
       —Cuando los cholos se dieron cuenta que Antonio se
       largaba con la pelota, le gritaron a uno que lo persiguiera:
       ¡qué trome corriendo el negrito! A mitad de pampa lo
       agarró y ya no pude ver más porque . . .
       Block quinto, escalera b, segundo piso:
       —En cuanto los cholos vieron que Antonio quedaba arre-
       glado, se fueron sobre nosotros . . .
       —¿No habías dicho que ustedes eran más?
       —Sí . . . pero ellos, no sé, asustaban con su sola pinta. Nos
       dimos cuenta y, ¡zas!, echamos a correr.
       —¿Hacia acá?
       —No, no podíamos; el arco de ellos quedaba hacia este lado
       y todos nosotros estábamos agrupados más bien hacia
       Lima . . .
       —¿Se fueron para allá?
       —Sí, claro; pero nos empezaron a apedrear y a mi me cayó
       una en la cabeza. Cerca de la pista nos rodearon y a patada y
       a puñete limpio . . .
       Block segundo, escalera b, tercer piso:
       —Nos estaban sacando el alma cuando pasó un patrullero.
       En seguida, violento, los cholos nos pegaron con más fuerza
       que antes . . .

*Notes, Bibliography, and Index*

# NOTES

## CHAPTER I

1   For those not familiar with *modernismo,* it should be noted
    that it was Latin America's original contribution to world
    literature. European influences, particularly French, were, of
    course, evident; but the *modernistas* were able to blend these
    foreign currents in such a way that the end product was
    peculiarly American. *Modernismo* began in the late 1870's as
    a literature of escape based on the "art for art's sake"
    esthetic. Through the use of vivid imagery and symbolism,
    the *modernistas* created a new style which effectively cap-
    tured not only surface beauty but also delicate moods and
    shades of meaning. As such, it constituted a strong reaction
    against the stodgy style and pedestrian themes associated
    with Romanticism. The leading exponent of *modernismo* was
    Rubén Darío; his *Azul* (1888) is a prime example of the first
    stage of the movement. In the final stage of *modernismo,* the
    writers were able to combine their stylistic concerns with an
    appreciation of the American scene and its problems. Darío's
    *Cantos de vida y esperanza* (1905) is an excellent example of
    this final phase. The movement lasted until just before World
    War I.
       In comparison with other Latin American countries, the
    manifestations of *modernismo* in Peruvian literature were
    quite tardy, despite the early prose and poetry contributions
    of Manuel González Prada, who is generally recognized by
    literary historians as a significant precursor of that movement.
    For comments on the relatively late appearance of *modern-
    ismo* in Peru, see Luis Alberto Sánchez, *Chocano poesía*
    (Lima: Editorial San Marcos, 1959), pp. 40–45; and Alberto
    Escobar, *La narración en el Perú* (Lima: Editorial Letras
    Peruanas, 1956), p. xvii.

2   Palma's *Cuentos malévolos* was first published in 1904 in Barcelona by Imprenta Salvat y Ca. Since the 1904 edition was not available to me, I have translated this passage from the most recent edition based on it: *Cuentos malévolos* (Lima: Editorial Nuevos Rumbos, 1959), p. 7.

3   See, for example, the following comments made by José Gálvez, a well-known Peruvian literary figure: "Besides his literary production, Don Ricardo Palma had the immense good fortune of fathering two children, Clemente and Angelica, to be the perpetuators of his great genius. And both of them, each in his own way (although a superficial observation of Clemente may cause one to think otherwise on occasion), have inherited, as their love of fiction and their creative abilities demonstrate, many of their father's most characteristic qualities." I have translated this quote from an article by Virgil A. Warren, "La obra de Clemente Palma," *Revista Iberoamericana*, No. 3 (April, 1940), 161.

4   Clemente Palma, "Datos bibliográficos sobre Clemente Palma," *Boletín de la Biblioteca de la Universidad Mayor de San Marcos*, VIII (July, 1938), 160–61.

5   *Cuentos malévolos* (Paris: Librería Paul Ollendorff, 1923). This edition will be used for all following quotations from the collection.

6   *Historietas malignas* (Lima: Editorial Garcilaso, 1924). Palma wrote other short stories which have never been collected in book form.

7   Quoted from Haakon M. Chevalier, *The Ironic Temper, Anatole France and His Time* (New York: Oxford University Press, 1932), p. 66.

8   *Dos tesis* (Lima: Imprenta de Torres Aguirre, 1897).

9   *Excursión literaria* (Lima: Imprenta de "El Comercio," 1894).

10  See A. E. Carter, *The Idea of Decadence in French Literature, 1830–1900* (Toronto: University of Toronto Press, 1958), p. 15. In this excellent study, the author points out that the feeling that the modern world was corrupt and sick was not limited to a few eccentrics, but was the firm opinion of nearly all authors, philosophers, and critics. Mr. Carter's general observations of the idea of decadence have been extremely helpful to me in formulating parts of this chapter.

11  The decadent hero par excellence of Huysmans' novel *A Rebours*. For an excellent study of decadent heroes in French literature, see George Ross Ridge, *The Hero in French*

*Decadent Literature* (Athens: University of Georgia Press, 1961).

12   Typical French decadent novels by Jean Lorrain, Villiers de l'Isle-Adam, and Joséphin Péladan, respectively.

13   One of the most striking and comprehensive pronouncements concerning the cult of artificiality in Latin American literature is embodied in a poem by Julián de Casal, entitled "En el campo."

14   See Carter, *The Idea of Decadence*, p. 6. In the fusion of the artificial and the modern, Carter notes a uniting of two fundamentally opposed ideas—a hatred of modern civilization and a love for the refinements which modern civilization has made possible. He comments: "Since decadent sensibility never resolved this contradiction, the movement suffered throughout its lifetime from a sort of literary schizophrenia. The decadent writers were all dutiful aesthetes; they inherited Romanticism's contempt for the bourgeois doctrines of the nineteenth century . . . and they had a quite legitimate horror of their own for the mediocrity of the century's official art. Yet as practitioners of decadence, they were obliged to wax enthusiastic over certain results of industrialism, results which allowed man to live more and more divorced from his natural state."

15   For further discussion of Des Esseintes, see Carter, *The Idea of Decadence*, pp. 20, 86–87.

16   *The Idea of Decadence*, pp. 4–5.

17   For further development of this idea, see Carter, *The Idea of Decadence*, p. 25.

18   Palma made this revealing statement concerning the fatal search for new sensations and pleasures which ultimately leads to death: "Today, with the Latin race leading the way, humanity journeys on, with its soul tormented by doubt, its nervous system wracked by intense and voluptuous shudderings, and its brain filled with curiosity, to regions . . . of madness and epilepsy. It is no longer able to stop itself; all of the past centuries thrust it forward; all of those centuries during which the old pleasures of life were exhausted impel humanity onward, in a frantic search for new ones, even though these may only be found in the last agonies of death. No matter; with death, as Guyau says, will come our last curiosity." I have translated this quote from Ventura García Calderón's *Del romanticismo al modernismo* (Paris: Librería Paul Ollendorff, 1910), pp. 458–59.

19   According to those who knew him, Palma was an avid reader

of Poe's works. One wall of Palma's study was dominated by a
large picture of the American author.

Poe's influence is evident in the characters, settings, and
themes of a few of Palma's narratives, particularly in "La
granja blanca" (*Cuentos malevolos*). Cordelia, the heroine
of Palma's story, is a physical and spiritual composite of Poe's
famous feminine characters Morella and Ligeia. The eerie
setting of Palma's story, an isolated, decaying rural mansion,
has its counterparts in Poe's "Ligeia" and "The Fall of the
House of Usher." At the close of the narrative, the familiar
conflagration of the morbid dwelling also takes place. Even
more interesting, however, is the development of a theme
which is basically that of "Morella" and "Ligeia": the
apparent return of the heroine, after her physical death, in
the form of another person. The similarity is particularly
striking in the case of "Morella," where it is implied that the
protagonist returns in the person of her own daughter. In this
story, Poe allows the daughter to mature before her death
and the macabre indication of her true identity. Palma alters
the time sequence by specifically attesting to the daughter's
identity while she is still a child. In addition, there are other
plot variations as Palma weaves an original tale in his own
right. Nevertheless, the basic similarities in setting, character,
and theme are obvious.

Other stories which show Poe's influence are "Mors ex
vita" and "Aventura del hombre que no nació" (*Historietas
malignas*). The first story is a composite of several of Poe's
tales of mesmerism, the spirit world, and other gothic horrors.
The second tale tells of a man's losing struggle to preserve his
identity which is being usurped by a stranger who is his
double in almost every respect, including name. It is similar
in theme to Poe's "William Wilson," including the fact that
both narrators tell of their ultimate destruction.

Like Poe, Palma was intrigued by the rare, the inexplicable, the supernatural, and exploited the literary possibilities
inherent in these elements. However, he introduced additional elements of irony and cruelty of which Poe was
incapable. Thus, at the same time that Poe's occasional
influence is recognized, the fact must not be overlooked that
Palma added to this inspiration a distinctive personal touch.

See also Ernesto More, "Capitulo en que se describe la
figura personalísma de Clemente Palma," *1951*, January 22,
1951, pp. 13–14.

20   For a further discussion of these criteria, see Austin Mc-
Giffert Wright, *The American Short Story in the Twenties*

(Chicago: University of Chicago Press, 1961), pp. 276–362.

21  Wright, *The American Short Story*, p. 290.

### CHAPTER II

1  The Indian has become one of the most significant figures in Peruvian literature during the course of the twentieth century. Using only the major landmarks, we can trace his literary appearance back to 1609 with the first part of El Inca Garcilaso's *Comentarios reales*, a treasure trove of information on the history, customs, traditions and religion of the Inca empire. In the eighteenth century, Indianist literature is limited to popular *romances;* but during the nineteenth century the Indian appears in Peruvian literature more frequently than before. Ricardo Palma, for example, in the *tradiciones* which he published between 1863 and 1899 included several with Indian themes which, for the most part, were prehispanic evocations. Other authors who used Indian themes include: Carlos Augusto Salaverry in a drama, *Atahualpa* (1875); Ricardo Rossell in the poems *Hima Sumac* (1877) and *Catalina Tupac Roca* (1879); and Nicolás de la Roca Vergallo, also a poet, in *La mort d'Atahualpa* (1870) and *Le livre des Incas* (1879). As is to be expected in view of the esthetic tastes of the time, the Indian appears as an exotic and legendary character with little or no relationship to reality.

   *Aves sin nido* (1889) by Clorinda Matto de Turner is one of the most significant contributions to the Indianist literature of Peru and all Latin America. A curious mixture of realism and romanticism, this novel has been called the first literary expression of social protest against the oppression of the Indian by his white overlords. Matto de Turner's description of the indignities suffered by the natives of the sierra is authentic, but her portrayal of this people is loaded with sentimentalism and betrays a basic misunderstanding of their character.

   Besides the works of Valdelomar, López Albújar, and García Calderón, the most notable examples of Indianist literature in the early years of the twentieth century are found in Chocano's poetry (*Alma américa*, 1906), a few of González Prada's essays (*Nuestros indios*, 1904), and a collection of poems by César Vallejo (*Los heraldos negros*, 1918).

2  Quoted from Luis Fabio Xammar, *Valdelomar: signo* (Lima: Ediciones Sphinx, 1940), p. 10.

3  I am indebted for this relatively unknown bibliographical item to Estuardo Núñez. See his introduction to Abraham Valdelomar's *La ciudad muerta, Crónicas de Roma* (Lima: Publicaciones de la Universidad Nacional de San Marcos, 1960), p. 13.

4  For additional details, see Augusto Tamayo Vargas, *Valdelomar, cuento y poesía* (Lima: Publicaciones de la Universidad Nacional de San Marcos, 1959), p. 11.

5  The following is a revealing quotation from one of the letters written to Enrique Bustamante Ballivián: "but the memory of the land is so poignant, one feels so far away from his loved ones; the sky, the sea, the land, the trees, and even the people of that place are missed so very much." Translated from an unpublished dissertation by May Loh, "Valdelomar cuentista" (Universidad de San Marcos, 1953), p. 3.

6  The so-called *Colónida* group had among its better known members Federico More, Percy Gibson, Aguirre Morales, Enrique Carillo, Bustamante y Ballivián, Alberto Hidalgo, César Vallejo, and Antonio Garland.

7  Lima, Talleres de la Penitenciaría, 1918. The following quotations, however, are taken from a more recent and slightly abridged edition published in Lima by Ediciones Nuevo Mundo in 1960.

8  Lima, Euroforión, 1921. The following quotations are from this source.

9  Piura is often incorrectly given as his birthplace. The confusion probably results from the fact that he spent much of his early childhood there with his grandparents. López Albújar was born when his father was only twenty-two and his mother barely eighteen years of age. His parents were not formally married at the time of his birth, nor when he was sent to live with his grandparents. This stigma caused him difficulties at first in being accepted, especially by the aunt though, ironically, her own father had been illegitimate.

10  Lima, Imprenta Lux, 1924, p. 27.

11  See Ernesto More, "Enrique López Albújar, escritor, poeta y espadachín," *Excelsior*, CCXXII (March–April, 1953), 19.

12  See Mario Vargas Llosa, "Narradores peruanos, Enrique López Albújar," *El Comercio*, September 11, 1955, p. 9.

13  This poem appeared in *La Tunda*. The newspaper came under heavy attack because of the numerous articles of censure which appeared in its pages against the alleged military despotism of Morales Bermúdez and Cáceres.

14  López Albújar, then just twenty years old, spoke eloquently in his own behalf, and his release was cheered by the

courtroom spectators. For an interesting and complete account, see *El Comercio*, June 26, 1893.

15   Lima, Imprenta Gil, 1895.

16   See Eudicio Carrera Vargas, "El destacado escritor y magistrado Enrique López Albújar cumple hoy 80 años," *El Comercio*, November 23, 1952, p. 2. This commentator indicates that López Albújar was finally forced to cease publication of the paper because of threatened reprisals against his father.

17   In 1943 López Albújar was honored with a trip to the United States where he visited Washington, D.C., and New York, and gave a speech at Columbia University. In a chat with the writer, he expressed his admiration for the beauty and charm of Washington, but confessed a certain dislike for the skyscrapers, the size, and frenzied movement of New York.

18   López Albújar graciously placed this manuscript at my disposal for purposes of this study. The following stories in this collection were published in *El Comercio*: "La mujer Diógenes," 1899; "El triunfo del trovador," 1897; "La gran payasada," 1898; "Febrimorbo," 1898; "Amor proteo," 1899. The unpublished stories are: "Celos, odio y venganza," 1899; "Desdén vencido," 1899; "El final de una boda," 1900; "Fuera de combate," 1900; "Una frase," 1901.

19   López Albújar also made this manuscript available to me. The following is a list of the stories contained in it: "Una expresión de agravios," 1915; "Castidad perdida," 1916; "Entre Scila y Caribdis," 1901; "El eterno expoliado," presumably written between 1904 and 1907; "La embajada de los perros," 1915; "Aquello vino de arriba," 1916; "Las dos carrozas," 1927; "El fin de un redentor," 1927. "El eterno expoliado" was published in López Albújar's own weekly, *El Amigo del Pueblo* of Piura, and "El fin de un redentor" was published in *Amauta*. The rest were published in *El Comercio*.

20   The title of the manuscript is easily explained. With one exception, the stories were written in Piura, a coastal town famous for its bright sunshine and broad expanses of sand.

21   Lima, Imprenta Mundial, 1920.

22   *Cuentos andinos*, 3rd ed. (Lima: Mejía Baca, 1950), p. 132. The following quotations are taken from this same edition.

23   Santiago de Chile, Ercilla, 1937.

24   Lima, Juan Mejía Baca and P. Villanueva, 1955.

25   The remaining three narratives of the book, "El señor de Echegoyen," "El maicito," and "La huelga que faltaba," are more closely related to López Albújar's vernacular production

since he turns for inspiration to less cosmopolitan and sophisticated types and settings. "El maicito," which Jiménez Borja in the preface terms the last of the "cuentos andinos," even seems out of place in the collection.

26  Paris, Henri Lefebvre, 1945.

27  Frances de Moimandre, "Ventura García Calderón," *El Comercio*, January 21, 1951, p. 17. In this article the author states: "It is a very rare thing even in a bilingual author. He writes as well in French as he does in Spanish. And this should not be taken as a compliment but as a statement of fact. He handles our language like a true master" (my translation).

28  Ventura García Calderón, *Dolorosa y desnuda realidad* (Paris: Garnier Brothers, 1914). Several commentators have mistakenly referred to this book as a novel.

29  Ventura García Calderón, *La venganza del cóndor* (Madrid: Mundo Latino, 1924).

30  For an interesting discussion of this type of story see Ray B. West, Jr., *The Short Story in America* (Chicago: Henry Regnery Co., 1952), pp. 92–94.

31  *Cuentos peruanos* (Madrid: Aguilar, 1952), p. 320. The cited edition is a fairly complete collection of his national short stories and will be used for subsequent quotations.

CHAPTER III

1  Some of Latin America's most famous regional novels were published during this period: *La vorágine* (1924), in which José Eustasio Rivera introduced the Amazon jungle area of Colombia; *Don Segundo Sombra* (1926), Ricardo Güiraldes' portrayal of the Argentine pampa; and *Doña Bárbara* (1929), in which Rómulo Gallegos depicts the Venezuelan *llano*.

2  For a detailed study of the social and literary influence of González Prada, see Eugenio Chang-Rodríguez, *La literatura política de González Prada, Mariátegui y Haya de la Torre* (Mexico: Studium, 1957), pp. 51–125.

3  Authors who have written at length on the life and works of Mariátegui are Chang-Rodríguez, *La literatura política,* and María Wiesse, *José Carlos Mariátegui* (Lima: Hora del Hombre, 1945).

4  Because of a difference in their aims, Mariátegui broke with APRA and Haya de la Torre in 1928.

5  The history of *Amauta* can actually be divided into three epochs: September, 1926–May, 1927, in which nine issues were published; December, 1927–March, 1930, in which

twenty issues were published; and April, 1930–September, 1930, in which three issues were published.

6   Wiesse, *José Carlos Mariátegui*, p. 77.
7   It was Sabogal who suggested the title for the periodical, which is the Inca word for a wise man or seer.
8   Quoted from Chang-Rodríguez, *La literatura política*, p. 186.
9   *Ibid.*
10  Lima, Bustamante y Ballivián, 1933.
11  In reality, many of the selections from the last collection cannot be classified as short stories because of their very reduced length and lack of plot.
12  *Amauta*, January, 1927, pp. 30–33, and February, 1927, pp. 18–20.
13  In *Plantel de inválidos* (Madrid: Ed. Historia Nueva, 1928), pp. 9–45.
14  Lima, Bustamante y Ballivián, 1934.
15  Lima, Rosay, 1930.
16  *Coplas y guitarras*, Vol. I (Lima: Bustamante y Ballivián, 1949). *Estampas mulatas*, Vol. II (Lima: Bustamante y Ballivián, 1951).
17  José Diez-Canseco, *Estampas mulatas* (Santiago: Zig-Zag, 1938).
18  Lima, Bustamente y Ballivián, 1951. All quotations will come from the 1951 edition of *Estampas mulatas*.
19  The term *cholo*, used almost exclusively in Peru and Bolivia, is the equivalent of mestizo, signifying a person of Indian and Spanish blood. The term *zambo* refers to Negro-Indian or Negro-mestizo mixtures.
20  "The Criollo Outlook in the Mestizo Culture of Coastal Peru," *American Anthropologist*, Vol. 57 (1955), 109.
21  *Ibid.*, p. 110.
22  This story won first prize in a contest sponsored by the Argentine newspaper *La Prensa*. Interestingly enough, all of his friends who had read the manuscript of the story were uniformly negative in their reactions as Diez-Canseco tells us: "My friends and literary colleagues were unanimous in their unfavorable opinion of this story. The kindest thing they were able to say to me about it was that I had plagiarized scandalously from Ventura García Calderón" (translated from *Estampas mulatas*, p. 6).
23  Translated from Benjamín Carrión, *San Miguel de Unamuno, ensayos* (Quito: Casa de la cultura Ecuatoriana, 1954), p. 205.
24  *Doce novelas de la selva* (Lima: Editorial Perú Actual,

1934). A second edition of this book was recently published in which the title was slightly changed and the opening essay on the jungle was omitted; otherwise, the content is not altered: *Doce relatos de la selva* (Lima: Editorial Juan Mejía Baca, 1958). *Mar y playa* was published in Lima by Taller Gráfico de P. Barrantes in 1940. The stories in this collection appeared throughout the thirties in national and foreign periodicals. Many were signed with the pseudonyms Fernán Lemarine or Julian Grave. *Mar y playa* was republished in Lima in 1959 by Editorial Nuevos Rumbos. All of the quotations come from the 1959 printing.

25    Romero's most recent collection of short stories has an urban setting. The stories lack the dramatic force and technical skill of his first two works. See Fernando Romero, *Rosarito se despide y otros cuentos* (Santiago de Chile: Editorial del Pacífico, 1955).

26    Buenos Aires, Editorial Tor, 1939.

27    Lima, La Empresa Periodística S. A. "La Prensa," 1941.

28    Lima, Editorial Hora del Hombre, 1948. The following quotation is from this volume.

29    Francisco Vegas Seminario, *Chicha, sol y sangre, cuentos peruanos* (Paris, Desclée de Brouwer, 1946). It is interesting to note that prior to this volume, his only writing experience had been limited to a few articles and poems in the Peruvian newspapers *El Tiempo* and *La Industria*. Vegas has since become a prolific writer of novels.

30    See Mario Vargas Llosa, "Francisco Vegas Seminario," *El Comercio*, September 18, 1955, p. 9.

31    Lima, Ministerio de Educación Pública, 1946. This collection was published in the same volume with *Cholerías*, by Porfirio Meneses, and *Tierras del alba*, by Francisco Izquierdo Ríos.

32    Lima, Ministerio de Educación Pública, 1946.

33    Lima, Ministerio de Educación Pública, 1946. See note 31.

34    Meneses published a second collection of short stories called *El hombrecillo oscuro y otros cuentos* (Lima: "La Crónica-Variedades" S. A., 1954). In these selections he enlarges his scope to include the coast, particularly Lima, as well as the sierra. He depicts a wide variety of characters including Negroes, Chinese, prostitutes, factory workers, and convicts. The stories are again based on a simple event or situation and, in some cases, the author carries it to the extreme of almost totally eliminating background material.

35    *Ande y selva* (Lima: Editorial Barrantes Castro, 1939).

36    Lima, Ministerio de Educación Pública, 1946. See note 31.

37    Lima, Editorial Selva, 1949.

38   *The Modern Psychological Novel* (New York: Grove Press, Inc., 1959), p. 11.

39   *Ibid.,* p. 14.

CHAPTER IV

1   There are English translations of two of Alegría's novels: *Broad and Alien Is the World,* trans. Harriet de Onís (New York: Farrar and Rhinehart, 1941) and *The Golden Serpent,* trans. Harriet de Onís (New York: Farrar and Rhinehart, 1943). José María Arguedas' award winning novel is *Los ríos profundos* (Buenos Aires: Editorial Losada, 1958).

2   Alegría's maternal grandmother, Juana Lynch de Bazán, had a decisive influence on his childhood. The stories, legends, and anecdotes which she related about the region gave him a rich knowledge of the beliefs, customs, and psychology of the people he later wrote about. During his adolescence, Alegría spent time with Manuel Baca, an Indian, who told him much about Quechua folklore.

3   *La serpiente de oro* (Santiago de Chile: Editorial Nascimento, 1935). *Los perros hambrientos* (Santiago de Chile: Zig-Zag, 1938). *El mundo es ancho y ajeno* (Santiago de Chile: Ercilla, 1941).

4   *Novelas completas* (Madrid: Aguilar, 1959), pp. 117–24. It is interesting to note that this same episode is included as one of the selections in a collection of Peruvian short stories: Armando Bazán, *Antología del cuento peruano* (Santiago de Chile: Zig-Zag, 1942), pp. 230–36.

5   For a complete study of the intercalated stories in this novel, see Enrique Normand Sparks, "Una observación sobre Los Perros Hambrientos," *Mercurio Peruano,* año XXX, No. 335, pp. 128–35. Sparks has noted that the five stories appear in arithmetic progression: The first two stories are separated by one chapter; the second and third stories are separated by two chapters; the third and fourth by three chapters; and the fourth and fifth by four chapters.

6   The three episodes mentioned are found in *Novelas completas* on pp. 680–98, 752–73, and 788–819. The interpolated folktales are, by order of appearance in the novel, on pp. 513–14, 803–7, 852, and 884–89.

7   Lima, Populibros Peruanos, 1963.

8   *El sapo y el urubu* (Santiago de Chile: Zig-Zag, 1939). *El castillo de Maese Falco* (Santiago de Chile: Zig-Zag, 1940). *La leyenda del nopal* (Santiago de Chile: Zig-Zag, 1940).

9   "La piedra y la cruz," *Carteles,* in *La Habana,* March 6, 1955,

p. 76. The same story, slightly revised, is included in *Duelo de caballeros* under the title, "La ofrenda de piedra." I am quoting from the earlier version which, in my opinion, is stylistically superior.

10   It is probable that "La madre" is based on a youthful experience of the author. He worked for awhile during 1923 in the jungle region of Marcabal Grande.

11   *Duelo de caballeros,* pp. 25 and 28.

12   Arguedas taught for a short while after his graduation from the university at a small school in Sicuani. There he spent many of his free hours giving special lessons to the Indians.

13   Some of his work in this field has been published in book form: José María Arguedas, *Canciones y cuentos del pueblo quechua* (Lima: Editorial Huascarán, 1949). For an English translation of some of the Quechua poetry and folktales collected by Arguedas, see Ruth Stephan, *The Singing Mountaineers, Songs and Tales of the Quechua People* (Austin: University of Texas Press, 1957).

14   *Agua* (Lima: CIP, 1935); *Yawar fiesta* (Lima: CIP, 1941); *Diamantes y pedernales* (Lima: Editorial Mejía Baca and Villanueva, 1954); *Los ríos profundos* (Buenos Aires: Editorial Losada, 1958); *El sexto* (Lima: Editorial Mejía Baca, 1961).

15   Arguedas expressed these feelings in a special introduction to *Diamantes y pedernales,* p. 6. All subsequent quotations are taken from this work.

16   Arguedas' personal satisfaction with the results of his efforts is best seen in his own words about *Agua:* "Six months later I opened the pages of the first story of *Agua.* There was no longer any complaint. That was the world as I knew it! The little village situated under a sky which was at once high, miserly, beautiful, and cruel; a little village burning with the fire of love and hatred, bathed in sun and silence, and serenaded by birds hidden in the trees. Would I succeed in conveying to others the real essence of that world? Would they feel the extreme passions of the people who inhabited it: their great sorrow, the incredible and transparent happiness with which they are accustomed to sing during their moments of rest? It seems so." (Translated from *Diamantes y pedernales,* p. 7).

CHAPTER V

1   *Lima, hora cero* (Lima: Tip. Peruana, 1954). A second edition of this collection was published in Lima by Populibros Peruanos

in 1964. All quotations are taken from the first edition. *Kikuyo* (Lima: Tip. Peruana, 1955).

2   *Barriada* is the name applied to the slum areas mushrooming at an alarming rate in the peripheral areas of Lima, as a result of a steady influx of people from the rural areas. The migrants are forced to squat on unoccupied land on the outskirts of the city where they construct miserable huts and shanties. Without benefit of running water or minimal hygienic standards, these people live in poverty, immorality, and hopelessness. Other large Latin American cities also face this troublesome phenomenon.

3   Lima, Círculo de Novelistas Peruanos, 1956. His most recent collections of short stories are *Las botellas y los hombres* (Lima: Populibros Peruanos, 1964) and *Tres historias sublevantes* (Lima: Editorial Mejía Baca, 1964). The first collection deals with the problems of urban dwellers; the stories in the second collection have rural settings.

4   Sebastián Salazar Bondy, *Náufragos y sobrevivientes* (Lima: P. L. Villanueva, 1954).

5   Lima, Nuevos Rumbos, 1958.

6   "El fugitivo" appeared in *El Comercio*, January 31, 1954, p. 1.

7   Lima, Letras Peruanas, 1954. Two other collections, both of which contain selections from *La batalla,* are *El Cristo Villenas* (Mexico: Los Presentes, 1956) and *Unas manos violentas* (Lima: Ediciones Peruanas, 1958). His most recent collection of stories is *Vestido de luta* (Lima: Editorial Mejía Baca, 1961). It does not measure up artistically to his previous works.

8   For an excellent study of these ideas in the short stories of Hemingway and Faulkner see Ray B. West, Jr., *The Short Story in America* (Chicago: Henry Regnery Company, 1952), pp. 82–102.

9   *Nahuín* (Lima: Ausonia, 1953). *Taita Cristo* (Lima: Populibros Peruanos, 1964).

10  For an excellent study of these two techniques and of the whole matter of stream-of-consciousness fiction see Robert Humphrey, *Stream of Consciousness in the Modern Novel* (Berkeley: University of California Press, 1962).

11  Translated from Alberto Escobar's *La narración en el Perú* (Lima: Editorial Letras Peruanas, 1956), p. 282.

12  *Stream of Consciousness,* p. 63.

# BIBLIOGRAPHY

## PRIMARY SOURCES

Alegría, Ciro. *La serpiente de oro.* Santiago de Chile: Ed. Nascimento, 1935.

———. *Los perros hambrientos.* Santiago de Chile: Ed. Zig-Zag, 1938.

———. *El mundo es ancho y ajeno.* Santiago de Chile: Ed. Ercilla, 1941.

———. "La piedra y la cruz," *Carteles,* in *La Habana,* March 6, 1955, pp. 74–76 and 113.

———. *Novelas completas.* Madrid: Aguilar, 1959.

———. *Duelo de caballeros.* Lima: Populibros Peruanos, 1963.

Arguedas, José María. *Agua.* Lima: CIP, 1935.

———. *Yawar fiesta.* Lima: CIP, 1941.

———. *Canciones y cuentos del pueblo quechua.* Lima: Ed. Huascarán, 1949.

———. *Diamantes y pedernales.* Lima: Ed. Mejía Baca y Villanueva, 1954.

———. *ríos profundos.* Buenos Aires: Ed. Losada, 1958.

———. *El sexto.* Lima: Ed. Mejía Baca, 1961.

Bazán, Armando. *Antología del cuento peruano.* Santiago de Chile: Ed. Zig-Zag, 1942.

Burga Freitas, Arturo. *Ayahuasca, mitos y leyendas del Amazonas.* Buenos Aires: Ed. Tor, 1939.

Churata, Gamaniel. "El gamonal," *Amauta,* January, 1927, pp. 30–33, and February, 1927, pp. 18–20.

Congrains Martín, Enrique. *Lima hora cero.* Lima: Tip. Peruana, 1954.

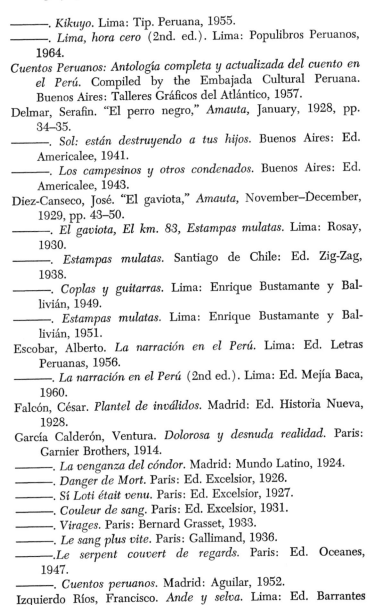

————. *Kikuyo.* Lima: Tip. Peruana, 1955.

————. *Lima, hora cero* (2nd. ed.). Lima: Populibros Peruanos, 1964.

*Cuentos Peruanos: Antología completa y actualizada del cuento en el Perú.* Compiled by the Embajada Cultural Peruana. Buenos Aires: Talleres Gráficos del Atlántico, 1957.

Delmar, Serafín. "El perro negro," *Amauta,* January, 1928, pp. 34–35.

————. *Sol: están destruyendo a tus hijos.* Buenos Aires: Ed. Americalee, 1941.

————. *Los campesinos y otros condenados.* Buenos Aires: Ed. Americalee, 1943.

Diez-Canseco, José. "El gaviota," *Amauta,* November–December, 1929, pp. 43–50.

————. *El gaviota, El km. 83, Estampas mulatas.* Lima: Rosay, 1930.

————. *Estampas mulatas.* Santiago de Chile: Ed. Zig-Zag, 1938.

————. *Coplas y guitarras.* Lima: Enrique Bustamante y Ballivián, 1949.

————. *Estampas mulatas.* Lima: Enrique Bustamante y Ballivián, 1951.

Escobar, Alberto. *La narración en el Perú.* Lima: Ed. Letras Peruanas, 1956.

————. *La narración en el Perú* (2nd ed.). Lima: Ed. Mejía Baca, 1960.

Falcón, César. *Plantel de inválidos.* Madrid: Ed. Historia Nueva, 1928.

García Calderón, Ventura. *Dolorosa y desnuda realidad.* Paris: Garnier Brothers, 1914.

————. *La venganza del cóndor.* Madrid: Mundo Latino, 1924.

————. *Danger de Mort.* Paris: Ed. Excelsior, 1926.

————. *Sí Loti était venu.* Paris: Ed. Excelsior, 1927.

————. *Couleur de sang.* Paris: Ed. Excelsior, 1931.

————. *Virages.* Paris: Bernard Grasset, 1933.

————. *Le sang plus vite.* Paris: Gallimand, 1936.

————. *Le serpent couvert de regards.* Paris: Ed. Oceanes, 1947.

————. *Cuentos peruanos.* Madrid: Aguilar, 1952.

Izquierdo Ríos, Francisco. *Ande y selva.* Lima: Ed. Barrantes Castro, 1939.

————. *Tierra del alba.* Lima: Ministerio de Educación Pública, 1946.

————. *Selva y otros cuentos.* Lima: Ed. Selva, 1949.

————. *Cuentos del Tío Doroteo.* Lima: Ed. Selva, 1950.

López Albújar, Enrique. *Miniaturas.* Lima: Imp. Gil, 1895.

————. "La mujer Diógenes, cuentos de mi juventud." Unpublished collection of short stories. Lima, 1899–1901.

————. "Cuentos de arena y sol." Unpublished collection of short stories, Lima, 1901–27.

————. *Cuentos andinos.* Lima: Imp. Mundial, 1920.

————. *Cuentos andinos* (2nd ed.). Lima: Imp. Lux, 1924.

————. *De mi casona.* Lima: Imp. Lux, 1924.

————. *Nuevos cuentos andinos.* Santiago de Chile: Ed. Ercilla, 1937.

————. *Cuentos andinos* (3rd ed.). Lima: Ed. Mejía Baca, 1950.

————. *Las caridades de la señora de Tordoya,* Lima: Ed. Mejía Baca y Villanueva, 1955.

————. *De mi casona* (2nd ed.). Lima: Primer Festival del Libro Peruano, 1958.

Macedo, María Rosa. *Ranchos de caña.* Lima: La Empresa Periodística, S. A. "La Prensa," 1941.

————. *Hombres de tierra adentro.* Lima: Ed. Hora del Hombre, 1948.

Manzor, Antonio R. *Antología del cuento hispanoamericano.* Santiago de Chile: Ed. Zig-Zag, 1939.

Meneses, Porfirio. *Cholerías.* Lima: Ministerio de Educación Pública, 1946.

————. *El hombrecillo oscuro y otros cuentos.* Lima: "La Crónica-Variedades," S. A., 1954.

Monguió, Luis. *La poesía postmodernista peruana.* Mexico: Fondo de Cultura Económica, 1954.

Nuñez, Estuardo (ed.). *Los mejores cuentos peruanos.* Lima: Empresa Gráfica T. Scheuch, 1956.

Paláez Bazán, Alfonso. *Cuando recién se hace santo.* Lima: Ministerio de Educación Pública, 1946.

————. *Tierra mía.* Lima: Ministerio de Educación Pública, 1946.

Palma, Clemente. *Excursión literaria.* Lima: Imprenta de "El Comercio," 1895.

————. *Cuentos malévolos.* Barcelona: Imp. Salvat y Ca., 1904.

————. *Cuentos malévolos* (2d ed.). Paris: Librería Paul Ollendorf, 1923.

————. *Historietas malignas.* Lima: Ed. Garcilaso, 1925.

————. *Cuentos malévolos* (3d ed.). Lima: Ed. Nuevos Rumbos, 1959.

Ribeyro, Julio. *Los gallinazos sin plumas.* Lima: Círculo de Novelistas Peruanas, 1956.

————. *Cuentos de circunstancias.* Lima: Ed. Nuevos Rumbos, 1958.

————. *Las botellas y dos hombres.* Lima: Populibros Peruanos, 1964.

————. *Tres historias sublevantes.* Lima: Ed. Mejía Baca, 1964.

Romero, Emilio. *Balseros del Titicaca.* Lima: Enrique Bustamante y Ballivián, 1934.

Romero, Fernando. *Doce novelas de la selva.* Lima: Ed. Perú Actual, 1934.

————. *Mar y playa.* Lima: Taller Gráfico de P. Barrantes, 1940.

————. *Rosarito se despide y otros cuentos.* Santiago de Chile: Ed. del Pacífico, 1955.

————. *Doce relatos de la selva.* Lima: Ed. Mejía Baca, 1958.

————. *Mar y playa.* Lima: Ed. Nuevos Rumbos, 1959.

Salazar Bondy, Sebastián. *Náufragos y sobrevivientes.* Lima: Ed. P. L. Villanueva, 1954.

Sueldo Guevara, Rubén. "El fugitivo," *El Comercio,* January 31, 1954, p. 1.

Valdelomar, Abraham. "Acción de gracias a los paisajes peruanos," *Sudamérica,* December 7, 1918 (no pagination).

————. *El caballero Carmelo.* Lima: Talleres de la Penitenciaría, 1918.

————. "El hipocampo de oro," *Stylo,* April 1, 1920.

————. *Los hijos del sol.* Lima: Ed. Euroforión, 1921.

Vargas Llosa, Mario. *Los jefes.* Lima: Populibros Peruanos, 1963.

Vargas Vicuña, Eleodoro. *Nahuín.* Lima: Ed. Ausonia, 1953.

————. *Taita Cristo.* Lima: Populibros Peruanos, 1964.

Vegas Seminario, Francisco. *Chicha, sol y sangre, cuentos peruanos.* Paris: Desclée de Brouwer, 1946.

Wiesse, María. "El forastero," *Amauta,* April, 1928.

————. "El hombre que se parecía a Adolfo Menjou," *Amauta,* May, 1929.

———. "El veneno," *Amauta,* September–October, 1929.

———. *Nueve relatos.* Lima: Enrique Bustamante y Ballivián, 1933.

———. *Pequeñas historias.* Lima: Enrique Bustamante y Ballivián, 1951.

———. *Linterna mágica.* Lima: Enrique Bustamante y Ballivián, 1954.

———. *El pez de oro y otras historietas.* Lima: Sebastián Barranca, 1958.

Zavaleta, Carlos. *La batalla.* Lima: Ed. Letras Peruanas, 1954.

———. *El Cristo Villenas.* Mexico: Los Presentes, 1956.

———. *Unas manos violentas.* Lima: Ed. Peruanas, 1958.

———. *Vestido de luta.* Lima: Ed. Mejía Baca, 1961.

CRITICAL STUDIES AND REFERENCES

Aldrich, Earl M. "The Quechua World of José María Arguedas," *Hispania,* March, 1962, pp. 62–66.

———. "El don cuentístico de Ciro Alegría," *Hispanófila,* Núm. 19, 1963, pp. 49–59.

———. "Observations on the Contemporary Peruvian Short Story," *Journal of Inter-American Studies,* October, 1963, pp. 451–60.

Anderson Imbert, Enrique. *Historia de la literatura hispanoamericana.* Mexico: Fondo de Cultura Económica, 1957.

Angeles Caballero, César A. "Abraham Valdelomar," *La Crónica,* March 15, 1958, p. 6.

———. "Ventura García Calderón," *La Crónica,* November 2, 1959, p. 6.

Barbagelata, Hugo D. *La novela y el cuento en Hispanoamérica.* Montevideo: Enrique Miguez, 1947.

Barrantes, Emilio. "Sentido vital de nuestras regiones naturales," *Cultura Peruana,* September, 1941 (no pagination).

Baudouin, Julio. "La obra romanesca de Ventura García Calderón," *La Crónica,* March 5, 1958, p. 6.

Bazán, Armando. "Los ochenta y cuatro años de Enrique López Albújar," *El Comercio,* February 8, 1957, p. 2.

Beltroy, Manuel. "Homenaje a Abraham Valdelomar," *Cultura Peruana,* July, 1948 (no pagination).

Bourricaud, Francois. "Sociología de una novela peruana," *El Comercio,* January 1, 1958, p. 2.

Brown Prado, Oswaldo. "Enrique Congrains Martín, un mendicante glorioso," *La Crónica,* March 9, 1955, p. 2.

Bumpass, Faye L. "Ciro Alegría, novelista de América," *IPNA,* XIV (Lima, 1950), 44–50.

Calvo, Eduardo. "Abraham Valdelomar, un enamorado de Barranco," *La Crónica,* November 23, 1958, p. 6.

Carrera Vergara, Eudicio. "El destacado escritor y magistrado Enrique López Albújar cumple hoy 80 años," *El Comercio,* November 23, 1952, p. 2.

Carrión, Benjamín. "El relatista peruano, José Diez-Canseco," *Revista de las Indias,* IV (Bogotá, 1939), 564–81.

——. *San Miguel de Unamuno, ensayos.* Quito: Casa de la Cultura Ecuatoriana, 1954.

Carter, A. E. *The Idea of Decadence in French Literature, 1830–1900.* Toronto: University of Toronto Press, 1958.

Castillo Ríos, Carlos. "El Ventura que yo conocí," *El Comercio,* November 8, 1959, p. 2.

Castro Arenas, Mario. "El mundo personal de Ciro Alegría," *La Prensa,* January 24, 1960, p. 16.

Chang-Rodríguez, Eugenio. *La literatura política de González Prada, Mariátegui y Haya de la Torre.* México: Colección Studium, 1957.

Chevalier, Haakon M. *The Ironic Temper, Anatole France and His Time.* New York: Oxford University Press, 1932.

Chunga, L. F. "El creador del cuento peruano: Abraham Valdelomar," *La Nación,* November 2, 1953, p. 2.

Cisneros, Luis Jaime. "Zavaleta, nueva trama del relato," *Expreso,* January 26, 1962, p. 11.

Cium, David. "Abraham Valdelomar, socialista," *El Callao,* August 20, 1948.

Cometta Manzoni, Aída. *El indio en la poesía de América Española.* Buenos Aires: Joaquín Torres, 1939.

Crawford, William Rex. *A Century of Latin American Thought.* Cambridge: Harvard University Press, 1944.

Delgado, Luis Humberto. *Diálogos con Ventura García Calderón.* Lima: Torres Aguirre, 1949.

——. *Ventura García Calderón.* Lima: Ed. Latino América, 1947.

"Dr. Emilio Romero Padilla," *Revista del Instituto de Geografía,* I (Lima, 1954), 12–13.

Edel, Leon, *The Modern Psychological Novel.* New York: Grove Press, Inc., 1959.

Englekirk, John E. *Edgar Allan Poe in Hispanic Literature.* New York: Instituto Las Españas, 1934.

"Entrevista con Abraham Valdelomar," *Balnearios*, January 17, 1917, p. 1.

Escobar, Alberto. "El lenguaje en la serpiente de oro." Unpublished doctoral dissertation, Facultad de Letras, University of San Marcos, 1952.

Fabio Xammar, Luis. *Valdelomar: signo.* Lima: Ed. Sphinx, 1940.

García Calderón, Ventura. *Del romanticismo al modernismo.* Paris: Librería Paul Ollendorf, 1910.

Gómez de la Serna, Ramón. *Ventura García Calderón.* Geneva: A. Kundig, 1946.

González Castro, Esmeralda. "José Diez-Canseco, periodista, satírico y estampista criollo," *El Comercio,* March 4, 1952, p. 3.

Henestrosa, Andrés (ed.). *González Prada.* México: Ediciones de la Secretaría de Educación Pública, 1943.

"Homenaje a José Diez-Canseco," *La Prensa,* March 5, 1950, p. 3.

*Hommage a Ventura García Calderón.* Article by Yves Gandos. Paris: Henri Lefebvre, 1947.

Humphrey, Robert. *Stream of Consciousness in the Modern Novel.* Berkeley: University of California Press, 1962.

Jiménez Borja, José. *Cien años de literatura y otros estudios críticos.* Lima: Club del Libro Peruano, 1940.

―――. "En torno a Enrique López Albújar," *El Comercio,* April 26, 1953.

La Torre, Alfonso. "José María Arguedas," *El Comercio,* June 4, 1959, p. 9.

Leavitt, Sturgis E. *A Tentative Bibliography of Peruvian Literature.* Cambridge: Harvard University Press, 1932.

Lerch, Emil. "Semblanza de la personalidad de Ventura García Calderón, escritor y diplomático," *El Callao,* August 1, 1948, p. 4.

Llosa Pautrat, Jorge Guillermo. "Dos escritores piuranos, López Albújar y Vegas Seminario," *El Comercio,* October 17, 1958, p. 2.

―――. "Dos horas con la sombra viva de Ventura García Calderón," *El Comercio,* December 14, 1959, p. 2.

Loh, May. "Valdelomar, cuentista." Unpublished thesis, degree of *bachiller,* Facultad de Letras, University of San Marcos, 1953.

López Albújar, Enrique. "Recordando a Clemente Palma," *El*

*Comercio,* June 7, 1953, suplemento dominical, p. 2.

Macedo, María Rosa. "Nostalgia de Valdelomar," *La Crónica,* March 18, 1949, p. 6.

Mariátegui, José. *Siete ensayos de interpretación de la realidad peruana.* Lima: Ed. Amauta, S. A., 1958.

Martin, Percy Alvin. *Who Is Who in Latin America.* Stanford: Stanford University Press, 1935.

Matto de Turner, Clorinda. *Aves sin nido.* Cusco: Imprenta H. G. Rozas, 1948.

Meléndez, Concha. *La novela indianista en Hispanoamérica (1832–1889).* Madrid: Imprenta de la Librería y Casa Editorial Hernando, 1934.

Miró, César, "Una carta inédita de Abraham Valdelomar," *El Comercio,* May 18, 1952, p. 9.

Miró, Quesada Laos, Carlos. *Rumbo literario del Perú.* Buenos Aires: Emecé Editores, 1947.

Mistral, Gabriela. "Un maestro americano del cuento," *La Prensa.* February 7, 1949, p. 3.

Moimandre, Francis de. "Ventura García Calderón," *El Comercio,* January 21, 1951, p. 17.

More, Ernesto. "Capítulo en que se describe la figura personalísima de Clemente Palma," *1951,* III (January 15, 1951), 22.

———. "Capítulo en que se describe la figura personalísima de Clemente Palma," *1951,* IV (January 22, 1951), 13–14.

———. "Enrique López Albújar, escritor, poeta y espadachín," *Excelsior,* CCXXII (March–April, 1953).

———. "Evocando a José Sabogal con María Wiesse, la notable escritora," *La Crónica,* January 5, 1958, p. 2.

———. "Gamaniel Churata," *La Crónica,* March 2, 1958, p. 2.

Moreno Mendiguren, Alfredo. *Repertorio de noticias breves sobre personajes peruanos.* Madrid: J. Sánchez Ocana, 1956.

Mugaburu, Raúl de. "A los 25 años de la desaparición de dos grandes escritores Peruanos," *Revista Iberoamericana,* May, 1948, p. 294.

———. "Valdelomar en Nueva York," *Cultura Peruana,* LXVII (January, 1954), no pagination.

———. "Ventura García Calderón: ¡Salve!" *La Crónica,* October 29, 1959, p. 6.

Neira Samanez, Hugo. "Sebastián Salazar Bondy: ironía y sociedad," *Expreso,* October 2, 1962, p. 10.

———. "Lima en Sebastián," *Expreso,* March 23, 1964, p. 12.

Orbegoza, Manuel Jesús. "El mundo sigue siendo ancho y ajeno,"
  La Crónica, December 5, 1957, pp. 1, 23.

———. "Dos novelistas de América: Ciro Alegría y Jorge Icaza,"
  Cultura Peruana, CXV (January, 1958), 10–13.

Orrego, Antenor. "Ubicación de Ciro Alegría," La Tribuna,
  December 9, 1957, p. 4.

Oviedo, José Miguel. "Sobre la obra de Julio Ramón Ribeyro," El
  Comercio, May 10, 1964, p. 8.

———. "Vargas Vicuña: un fresco y trágico indigenismo." El
  Comercio, September 6, 1964, p. 6.

Oyague, Lucas. "Con un ruidoso juicio de imprenta inició D.
  Enrique López Albújar su vida literaria," Excelsior, CCVI
  (July–August, 1950), 19–23.

Palma, Clemente. "Datos bibliográficos sobre Clemente Palma,"
  Boletín de la Biblioteca de la Universidad Mayor de San
  Marcos, VIII (July, 1938), 158–62.

Palma, Ricardo. Flor de tradiciones. Introducción, selección, y
  notas de George W. Umphrey y Carlos García Prada. Mexico:
  Ed. Cultura, 1943.

Pastor, Alberto Enrique. "Abraham Valdelomar, estudiante secun-
  dario," La Nación, November 30, 1953, p. 2.

Pavletich, Estéban. "El homenaje a Enrique López Albújar," La
  Crónica, July 12, 1955, p. 7.

Paz Soldán, Carlos Enrique. "Ventura García Calderón," La
  Crónica, January 30, 1949, p. 4.

Porras Barrenechea, Raúl. Mito, tradición e historia del Perú.
  Lima: Imprenta Santa María, 1951.

Recavarren, Jorge Luis. "Ventura García Calderón," La Prensa,
  June 9, 1952, p. 3.

———. "Otra vez con nosotros, Ciro Alegría," La Prensa, January
  15, 1960, p. 18.

———. "José María Arguedas y Carlos Zavaleta," La Prensa,
  December 18, 1961, p. 10.

Ridge, George Ross. The Hero in French Decadent Literature.
  Athens: University of Georgia Press, 1961.

Rowe, John Howland. "Inca Culture," Handbook of South American Indians. Ed. by Julian H. Steward. Vol. II. Washington:
  Government Printing Office, 1946.

Russell, Dora Isella. "Ventura García Calderón," Apartado de
  Revista Nacional de Montevideo, CLXXX (1954), 5.

Salazar Bondy, Sebastián. "El caso de Congrains," La Prensa,
  February 14, 1955, p. 8.

————. "Ciro Alegría: realidad y compromiso," *La Prensa,* December 6, 1957, p. 12.

————. "Valdelomar, vuelco a sí mismo," *La Prensa,* January 14, 1959, p. 8.

————. "Ventura García Calderón, distancia y soledad," *El Comercio,* November 8, 1959, p. 4.

————. "Ribeyro, nueva perspectiva," *El Comercio,* May 31, 1964, p. 8.

Sanchez, Luis Alberto. *Don Manuel.* Santiago: Ed. Ercilla, 1937.

————. *América: novela sin novelistas.* Santiago de Chile: Ed. Ercilla, 1940.

————. *La literatura peruana, derrotero para una historia espiritual del Perú.* Vol. VI. Asunción del Paraguay: Ed. Guarania, 1951.

————. *Proceso y contenido de la novela hispanoamericana.* Madrid: Ed. Gredos, 1953.

————. *Chocano: poesía.* Lima: Ed. San Marcos, 1959.

Simmons, Ozzie G. "The Criollo Outlook in the Mestizo Culture of Coastal Peru," *American Anthropologist,* 57 (1955), 107–15.

Sparks, Enrique Normand. "Una observación sobre Los Perros Hambrientos," *Mercurio Peruano,* Núm. 335, pp. 128–35.

Stephan, Ruth. *The Singing Mountaineers, Songs and Tales of the Quechua People.* Austin: University of Texas Press, 1957.

Suárez Miraval, Manuel. "Cuentos andinos: páginas siempre legibles," *Idea,* VIII (August, 1950), 10.

Tamayo Vargas, Augusto. *Literatura Peruana.* 2 vols. Lima: Ed. "D. Miranda," 1953.

————. "El mar y la costa en Abraham Valdelomar," *Letras,* L–LIII (1954), 24, 27, 29.

————. *Valdelomar: cuento y poseía.* Lima: Publicaciones de la Universidad de San Marcos, 1959.

————. "Valdelomar y la semana santa," *El Comercio,* March 27, 1959, p. 2.

Tauro, Alberto. *Elementos de literatura peruana.* Lima: Ed. Palabra, 1946.

Torres de Vidaurre, José. "Valdelomar en Ica," *La Crónica,* July 30, 1958, p. 6.

Valcárcel, Luis E. *Mirador indio.* Cusco: Primer Festival del Libro Sur-Peruano, 1958.

Valle, Rafael Heliodoro. "Diálogo con Ventura García Calderón," *El Comercio,* August 19, 1951, p. 10.

Van Leisen, Herbert, *Ventura García Calderón, Un Athénien Sur le Pacifique.* Geneva: A. Kundig, 1944.

Vargas Llosa, Mario. "José María Arguedas," *El Comercio,* September 4, 1955, p. 8.

————. "Narradores peruanos, Enrique López Albújar," *El Comercio,* September 11, 1955, p. 9.

————. "Francisco Vegas Seminario," *El Comercio,* September 18, 1955, p. 9.

————. "María Weisse de Sabogal," *El Comercio,* October 2, 1955, p. 9.

————. "María Rosa Macedo," *El Comercio,* October 23, 1955, p. 9.

————. "Arturo Burga Freitas," *El Comercio,* November 20, 1955, p. 9.

————. "Emilio Romero," *El Comercio,* June 2, 1957, p. 4.

Vargas Prada, Julio. "El arte narrativo de Ciro Alegría," *La Crónica,* July 26, 1955, p. 7.

Vásquez, Emilio. "Valdelomar, el escritor multiple," *Fanal,* XL (1954), 20–23.

Velásquez Neyra, José. "Novelista Ciro Alegria ha regresado al Perú," *La Prensa,* December 5, 1957, pp. 1, 8.

Vilariño de Olivieri, Matilde. *Las novelas de Ciro Alegría.* Santander: Taller de Artes Gráficas de los Hermanos Bedia, 1956.

Warren, Virgil A. "La obra de Clemente Palma," *Revista Iberoamericana,* April, 1940, p. 161.

West, Ray B., Jr. *The Short Story in America.* Chicago: Henry Regnery Co., 1952.

Wiesse, María. *José Carlos Mariátegui.* Lima: Hora del Hombre, 1945.

————. "Ciro Alegría: gran novelista de América," *La Crónica,* January 21, 1958, p. 6.

Wright, Austin McGiffert. *The American Short Story in the Twenties.* Chicago: University of Chicago Press, 1961.

Zubizarreta, Armando. "Literatura y experiencia vital en el caballero Carmelo," *El Comercio,* February 17, 1957, p. 2.

# INDEX

DATE DUE